Mighty Maps!

Facts, Fun and Trivia to Develop Map Skills

by Cindy Barden

illustrated by Chris Nye

Teaching & Learning Company

1204 Buchanan St., P.O. Box 10
Carthage, IL 62321

This book belongs to

_____

This book was developed for the Teaching & Learning Company
by The Good Neighbor Press, Inc., Grand Junction, CO.

Cover illustration by Chris Nye

Copyright © 1995, Teaching & Learning Company

ISBN No. 1-57310-037-4

Printing No. 98

Teaching & Learning Company
1204 Buchanan St., P.O. Box 10
Carthage, IL 62321

Table of Contents

Introduction to Maps
How to Use This Book/Resources.....................1
What Is a Map?.....................2
Mapmaking.....................3
Map Titles.....................4

Maps and Globes
Flat or Round?.....................5
Laying It Out Flat.....................6

Using an Atlas
Using an Atlas.....................7
Famous Places.....................8
Land and Water.....................9
The Continent of Antarctica.....................10

Directions
Which Way Is North?.....................11
North, South, East, West
    and Points In-Between.....................12
Which Way from Omaha?.....................13
Which Way to El Dorado?.....................14
X Marks the Spot.....................15
Pinpoint the State.....................16

Using a Map Grid
Finding Your Way Around a Map.....................17
Zap! You're in North Dakota.....................18
Grid Work.....................19

Latitude and Longitude
The Equator and Other Imaginary Lines.....................20
More Imaginary Lines.....................21
On a Flat Map.....................22
Pinpointing Places.....................23
Finding Places Around the World.....................24

Time Zones
What Time Is It?.....................25
Time Zones Across the United States.....................26

Map Scales and Distance
How Far?.....................27
Drawing a Map to Scale.....................29
As the Crow Flies.....................30

Direction and Distance
Colorado Vacation.....................31

Map Keys
Map Symbols: What Do They Mean?.....................32
Getting Around the Mall.....................33
Africa.....................34
The Continent of Africa Map.....................35
City Size.....................36
A Map of Somewhere Else:
    Application of Skills.....................37
Let's Visit Yellowstone National Park.....................38
Yellowstone National Park Map.....................39

Road Maps
Road Maps.....................40
Traveling Through Utah.....................41

Mileage Charts
Reading Mileage Charts.....................42

Political Maps
Political Maps.....................43
Switzerland, Indiana?.....................44
Where Is Switzerland When
    It's Not in Indiana?.....................45
The Continent of Europe Map.....................46
Asia, the Largest Continent.....................47
The Continent of Asia Map.....................48

City Maps
Turn Right on Yum Yum Street.....................49
Smalltown, U.S.A......................50
Smalltown, U.S.A. Map.....................51

Inset Maps
Meet Me in St. Louis, Louis.....................52
Using What You've Learned:
    Application of Skills.....................53

Physical Maps
Physical Maps.....................54
The Land Down Under.....................55
The Continent of Australia Map.....................56
How High Is Up?.....................57
Canada Map.....................58
The Highs and Lows.....................59
How Low Does It Go?.....................60
Mexico.....................61

Specialty Maps
Specialty Maps.....................62
A Look at South America.....................63
The Continent of South America Map.....................64
Lots of People.....................65
Comparison Maps.....................66
My How We've Grown!.....................67
Product Maps.....................69
Where Does All the Corn Grow?.....................70
Corn: An Important Crop Around the World.....................71
Weather Maps.....................72
Weather and Climate.....................73
How Hot Does It Get?.....................74
How Cold Does It Get?.....................75
Historical Maps.....................76
Historical Map of the United States.....................77
Would You Like to Buy the Brooklyn Bridge?.....................78
Sales Are Booming.....................79
Pizza Deluxe.....................80

Appendix
Know These Terms: Review Page.....................81
Challenge Questions.....................82
Suggestions for Using Maps.....................83
World Map: Two-Page World Map.....................84
U.S. Map: Two-Page U.S. Map.....................86
North America Map.....................88
South America Map.....................89
Answer Key.....................90

TLC10037 Copyright © Teaching & Learning Company, Carthage, IL 62321

Dear Teacher,

Welcome to *Mighty Maps!* Getting from here to there doesn't have to be a mystery—not when students learn to read the special language used on maps. As you tour the world through maps, Mr. Compass pops up to offer helpful hints, bits of trivia and encouragement.

Maps are everywhere, in the telephone book, on T-shirts, in magazines and newspapers, on stamps and even food labels. Collect as many maps as you can. Start a map file that students are free to browse through. Ask students to contribute maps to the file.

This book may be used as a supplement to other units in geography. Most activities are self-contained. Students will need an atlas or globe for reference to complete some activities. If you feel an activity is too difficult for your students, encourage them to work on it in small groups or as a class.

In *Mighty Maps!* students will:

- learn about early mapmaking
- compare globes to maps
- use an atlas
- use a compass
- make a compass
- find the four cardinal directions
- locate the four intermediate directions
- follow directions to locate various places
- read map scales
- measure distance using different scales
- practice drawing a map to scale
- use a number/letter grid to locate places
- use latitude and longitude to locate places
- identify political regions
- use time zone maps
- identify map symbols
- draw map symbols
- practice using city, state, country, continent and world maps
- draw their own maps
- follow directions on road maps
- use several types of physical maps
- use specialty maps including population density, weather and product maps
- prepare a historical map
- transfer information between a map and a graph

Check the "How to Use This Book" section on the next page for other helpful tips and ideas.

Enjoy your world tour. When students know the language of maps, they'll find they *can get there from here.*

Sincerely,

Cindy

Cindy Barden

How to Use This Book

The reproducible activities in *Mighty Maps!* are arranged in sequential order. Students use skills learned early in the book in activities that appear later. After learning new terms and concepts, students have an opportunity to practice the various map skills.

You will need a few supplies for some of the activities, specifically a globe, world atlas, U.S. atlas, compass, ruler, crayons, markers or colored pencils. To make the compass on page 11, students will need a short piece of string, a pencil, a needle, a magnet and a glass or jar wider than the length of the needle.

You'll find maps of the seven continents located in the book near an activity related to each continent. The appendix contains a two-page U.S. map and a two-page world map. Students will need copies of these maps for several activities in the book. You'll find other suggestions for using the maps in the appendix.

In addition, the appendix contains a one-page review of terms, a list of challenge questions and an answer key.

You and your students may find these books useful as you practice map skills:

Arnold, Caroline. *Maps and Globes: Fun, Facts and Activities.* Franklin Watts, 1984.

Berry, Marilyn. *help is on the way for: Maps & Globes.* Childrens Press, 1985.

Children's Atlas of the Universe. Rand McNally, 1990.

Cool Places, U.S.A. Rand McNally, 1994.

Hogan, Paula Z. *The Compass.* Walker and Company, 1982.

Kids' U.S. Road Atlas. Rand McNally, 1992.

Knowlton, Jack. *Maps & Globes.* Thomas Y. Crowell, 1985.

Lambert, David. *Maps and Globes.* Wayland, 1986.

Lehr, Paul E., R. Will Burnett, and Herbert S. Zim. *Weather.* Golden Press, 1991.

Picture Atlas of Our World. National Geographic Society, 1991.

Sipiera, Paul P. *Globes* (A New True Book). Childrens Press, 1991.

Taylor, Barbara. *Be Your Own Map Expert.* Sterling Publishing Co., Inc., 1994.

Weiss, Harvey. *Maps: Getting from Here to There.* Houghton Mifflin, 1991.

What Is a Map?

Maps are flat pictures of places as seen from above. They provide important information. Maps can tell you

> . . . how to get from one place to another
> . . . the distance between places
> . . . where places are located

What are three other types of information you can learn from a map?

_____

_____

_____

Maps can show a small area, like a room, a building or a neighborhood. They can include larger areas like a state, a country or the world.

Discussion Topic

If you don't drive a car, fly an airplane or sail a boat, what good are maps?

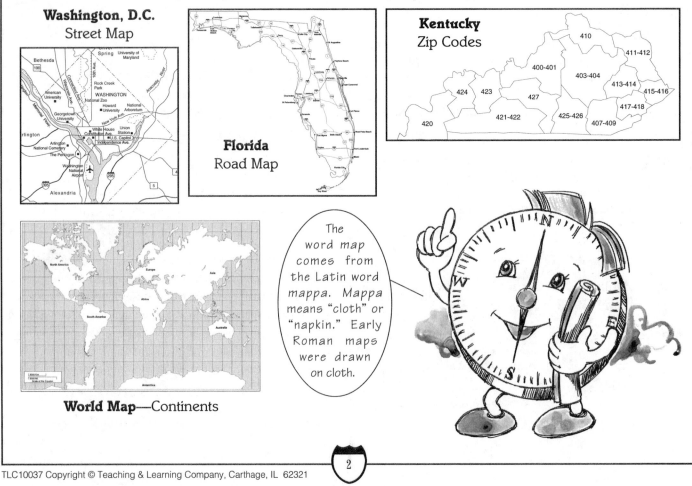

Washington, D.C.
Street Map

Florida
Road Map

Kentucky
Zip Codes

World Map—Continents

The word *map* comes from the Latin word *mappa*. *Mappa* means "cloth" or "napkin." Early Roman maps were drawn on cloth.

Mapmaking

If a map is a flat picture of an area as seen from above, how did early **cartographers** (mapmakers) draw maps?

Sailors drew maps as they sailed along coastlines. Some mapmakers drew maps based on what they saw while traveling or heard from other travelers. Another method was to climb a tall tree or a high mountain and look down. This gave the mapmaker a better view of a wider area.

Unfortunately, many early maps were not very detailed. Some were completely wrong. List some reasons why you think early mapmakers had problems making accurate maps.

_____

_____

Early maps were drawn on whatever material was available—clay tablets, animal hides, papyrus, cloth, tree bark, plant leaves and rocks.

If you were at the beach without paper or pencil, how could you draw a map to show someone how to get to a restaurant a mile away?

_____

_____

Over the centuries the shape of the Earth has been described as flat, cube-shaped, a cone, a cylinder, a spiral like a spring and a flat plain surrounded by a huge wall.

The Greek geographer, Ptolemy (87-150 A.D.), is credited with drawing the first maps showing a round Earth. Using copies of Ptolemy's maps, Christopher Columbus searched for a shortcut to the Spice Islands of India. Instead of sailing east around the entire continent of Africa, he thought he could sail west around the Earth. Problems arose because no one knew the true size of the Earth. Early cartographers thought the Earth was about 7,000 miles smaller than it really is.

Eskimos carved coastal maps on driftwood. They cut notches in the wood to show the size and shape of inlets and bays.

When people invented hot air balloons in the 1780s, they could finally see the Earth from above for much greater distances. How do you think the invention of airplanes helped mapmakers draw even more accurate maps?

_____

_____

_____

Map Titles

Most maps have titles. The **map title** tells you what types of information can be found on the map. A map title could simply describe the area shown on the map, like **The World**, **China**, **Nevada State Map** or **City Map of Paris**.

Map titles could also be more specific. For example, **Immigration to the New World 1600-1700** or **Average Rainfall in July in the British Islands**. When map titles are specific, you know what type of information you will find on the map.

Write map titles for each map described below. Keep titles short whenever possible, but be specific.

A map of Georgia that shows the annual production of peanuts in the state in 1995.

_____

A map of the country of India showing the amount of rainfall during the 1692 monsoon season.

_____

A map of New York City that shows places that tourists would be interested in visiting.

_____

A map that shows where people who watch MTV live.

_____

A map of the world showing the depth of the oceans and heights of the mountains.

_____

A map that shows where in New Mexico you would be most likely to find rattlesnakes.

_____

A world map showing where different types of dinosaurs lived during the Jurassic Period.

_____

A map that shows rain forests and wetlands in South America.

_____

By reading the title of a map, you'll know what type of information will be included.

A map of Asia that shows population growth during the last 10 years.

_____

A map showing major battlefields of the Civil War.

_____

Flat or Round?

Globes are three-dimensional models of the Earth. The location of land and water and the relative size of landforms can be shown more accurately on a globe than on a flat map. The distances between places is also more accurately shown on a globe.

Look closely at a globe. What types of information can you learn from a globe? What do the various colors represent?

Try It

An easy way to find the shortest route between two places on a globe is to use a piece of string.

Find Los Angeles, California, and Tokyo, Japan, on the globe. Tokyo appears almost directly west of Los Angeles. Put one end of the string on Los Angeles. Stretch it tightly between the two cities. You'll find that the shortest route is not directly west.

Check these other globe facts with string. Answer true or false.

1. Miami, Florida, and Portland, Oregon, are about the same distance from Stockholm, Sweden. _____

2. The most direct route from Chicago, Illinois, to Calcutta, India, would be over the North Pole. _____

3. The shortest way to get from New York to Tokyo would be by way of Fairbanks, Alaska. _____

All three answers are true. Now go to a flat world map. Use the string and look for the shortest routes between the places listed above. What did you find?

_____

_____

_____

My favorite book is *Around the World in 80 Days* by Jules Verne.

Although globes are more accurate than flat maps, there are several disadvantages to globes:

- A globe isn't a completely accurate picture of the Earth. Globes are round and smooth. The Earth bulges at the Equator. It is covered with mountains and valleys.

- Unless they are very, very large, it is impossible to show much detail on a globe.

- Globes are more difficult to carry around than flat maps.

Laying It Out Flat

Even though the Earth is round, most maps we use are flat. Although flat maps are much easier to carry in your pocket or purse, it is very difficult to draw a flat map of a round world. Flat maps are two-dimensional. The Earth is three-dimensional.

Think About It

Imagine drawing a map of the Earth on an orange. What would happen if you removed the peeling in one piece and tried to lay it out flat?

_____

This is the type of world map you would get if you tried to peel a globe like an orange and lay the pieces flat.

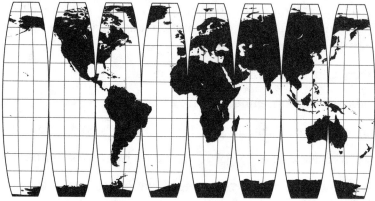

Imagine drawing a map of the Earth on an inflated balloon. What would happen if you cut the balloon and laid out the pieces, pulling and stretching them until they laid flat?

_____

This is the type of world map you would get if you stretched the pieces of a balloon flat.

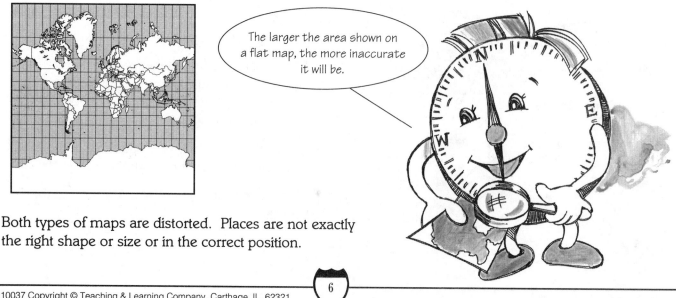

The larger the area shown on a flat map, the more inaccurate it will be.

Both types of maps are distorted. Places are not exactly the right shape or size or in the correct position.

Using an Atlas

An **atlas** is a book of maps. A world atlas contains maps of the seven continents and most countries. A U.S. atlas contains maps of each state. A city atlas contains detailed maps of cities.

Look through an atlas. What types of information can you find?

_____

_____

Use a world atlas to answer these questions:

1. What country lies directly above (north of) Spain?

   _____

2. On what continent would you find Mongolia?

   _____

3. On what continent would you find Morocco?

   _____

4. Is New Zealand closer to Australia or Japan?

   _____

5. What is the capital of Brazil?

   _____

6. What ocean is along the west coast of Mexico?

   _____

7. Does Afghanistan share a border with India?

   _____

8. What was the former name of Sri Lanka?

   _____

Use a U.S. atlas to answer these questions:

9. Which state is larger, California or Delaware?

   _____

10. What is the capital of Louisiana?

    _____

11. What two states border on Washington?

    _____ and _____

12. What body of water forms the coast of Maine?

    _____

13. Is Nebraska closer to Arizona or North Dakota?

    _____

14. What river runs between Arkansas and Tennessee?

    _____

15. Which four states share a border with Mexico?

    _____

16. Bismarck is the capital of which state?

    _____

The word *atlas* comes from the name of the Greek god, Atlas, who was forced to carry the Earth on his shoulders.

Famous Places

Use an atlas to find these natural and people-made landmarks. The state location is given as a clue. Use a copy of the U.S. map found at the back of this book. Write the letters in the correct locations on the map.

A.	Appomattox Court House	Virginia
B.	Carlsbad Caverns	New Mexico
C.	Crater Lake	Oregon
D.	Disneyland	California
E.	Golden Gate Bridge	California
F.	Grand Canyon	Arizona
G.	Great Salt Lake	Utah
H.	Great Smoky Mountains National Park	Tennessee/North Carolina
I.	Everglades National Park	Florida
J.	Hoover Dam	Nevada/Arizona
K.	Liberty Bell	Pennsylvania
L.	Mammoth Cave National Park	Kentucky
M.	Mauna Loa	Hawaii
N.	Mesa Verde	Colorado
O.	Mount McKinley	Alaska
P.	Mount Rushmore	South Dakota
Q.	Niagara Falls	New York
R.	Sears Tower	Illinois
S.	Statue of Liberty	New York
T.	Washington Monument	Washington, D.C.
U.	Yellowstone National Park	Wyoming

I'd like to visit the Mustard Museum in Mt. Horeb, Wisconsin.

List five other places in the United States you have visited or would like to visit. List the state where each place is located. Write the letter of the five places you selected on the map.

V. _____   _____

W. _____   _____

X. _____   _____

Y. _____   _____

Z. _____   _____

Select one of these famous places for a report. Illustrate your report or use pictures cut from newspapers and magazines.

Land and Water

Water covers 70% of the Earth. The rest of the Earth is covered by seven major land masses called **continents** and thousands of small islands.

Continent	Area in square miles
Africa	11,700,000
Antarctica	5,405,000
Asia	17,240,000
Australia	2,967,909
Europe	3,840,000
North America	9,410,000
South America	6,860,000

The coldest place in the world is at Polus Nedostupnosti, Antarctica, with an estimated average annual temperature of -72°F.

1. Which continent is the largest? _____

2. Which two continents are completely in the Southern Hemisphere?

_____ and _____

(Use a world atlas to find the answer.)

3. Which continent is the smallest? _____

Antarctica, the Coldest Continent

The continent of Antarctica is mostly uninhabited. Most of the continent lies within the Arctic Circle. A few thousand people live there during the warmest months, but only a few hundred stay year round. Snow and ice covers all but two to three percent of the continent permanently.

Although it contains no countries and no major cities, parts of Antarctica do have names and various countries claim the land. Use the map of Antarctica on the next page to fill in the blanks below.

4. Australia claims part of _____ Land, all of _____ Land, _____ Highland and

part of _____ Land.

5. France claims a small slice of _____ Land.

6. Norway claims parts of _____ Land and _____ Land.

7. New Zealand claims territory in _____ Land and the area around the _____ Ice Shelf.

8. Part of the land claimed by the United Kingdom is also claimed by which other two countries?

_____ and _____

The Continent of Antarctica

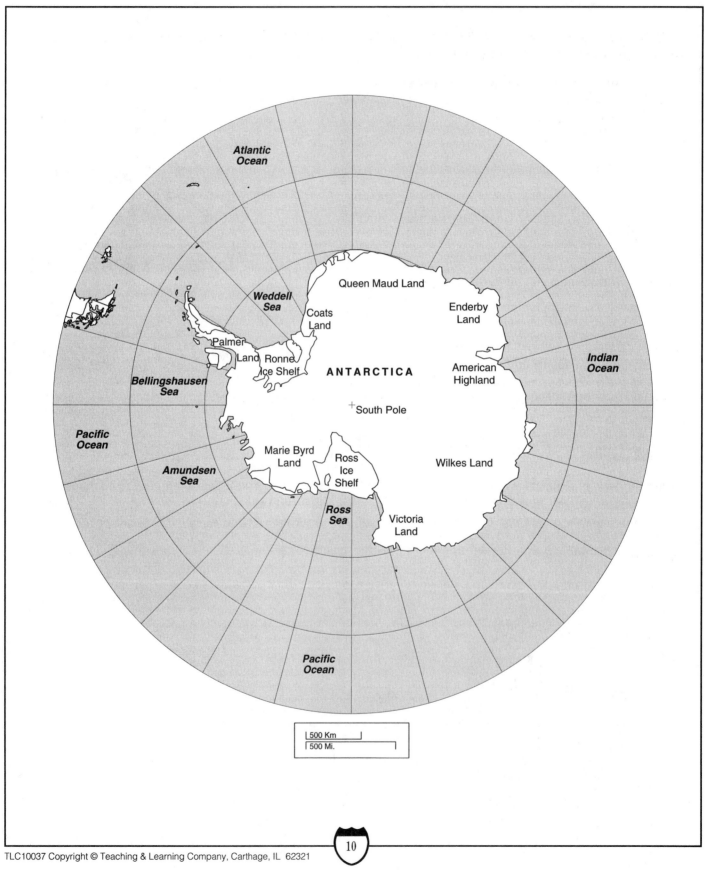

Which Way Is North?

Supplies needed for this activity: a compass, a short piece of string, a pencil, a needle, a magnet and a glass or jar wider than the length of the needle.

The sun rises in the east and sets in the west. At night, stars fill the sky. Early explorers and sailors told **direction** by watching the sun and the stars. But what happened when it was cloudy? They needed something more reliable. Using a piece of lodestone which is magnetic, a simple tool called a magnetic **compass** was invented. With a compass people always knew which direction was north.

Try It

Look at the needle of a compass. The needle always points to the north. No matter which way you turn the compass, the needle will always point in the same direction. Turn the compass until the needle lines up with the N. Stand so you are facing north. When you face NORTH, you can easily find SOUTH (behind you), EAST (to your right) and WEST (to your left).

Make Your Own Compass

Rub one end of a magnet along a needle about 30 times. Always rub in the same direction, towards the point, not back and forth. The end of the needle will become magnetized. Check your needle by using it to pick up a pin or paper clip. If it isn't magnetized yet, continue rubbing the magnet along the needle.

When the needle is magnetized, tie one end of a short piece of thread around the middle of the needle. Tie the other end around the middle of a pencil. Place the pencil across the rim of a glass so the needle hangs inside without touching the sides of the glass. When the needle stops moving, it will point in a NORTH-SOUTH direction.

Check your homemade compass with a real compass to see how accurate it is.

People are attracted to me because of my magnetic personality.

North, South, East, West and Points In-Between

When you face the sun as it rises, you are facing EAST. When you face the sun as it sets, you are facing WEST. Look at the compass below. Imagine standing at the center of the compass with your right hand pointing east. You would be facing NORTH. SOUTH would be behind you.

North, south, east and west are the four main directions we use.

1. If you are facing west, what direction is to your right? _____

2. If you are facing south, what direction is to your left? _____

3. If you are facing north, what direction is behind you? _____

4. If you are facing south, what direction is to your right? _____

Besides north, south, east and west, there are also in-between directions, called intermediate directions. The point between north and east is called northeast. Look at the compass below to learn the names of the other in-between directions.

A. What direction is halfway between east and south? _____

B. What direction is halfway between north and west? _____

C. What direction is halfway between south and west? _____

D. What direction is exactly opposite southeast? _____

These are the abbreviations used:

N = north   S = south

E = east   W = west

NE = northeast   NW = northwest

SE = southeast   SW = southwest

Which Way from Omaha?

Most maps use some type of symbol to show directions. North is usually at the top of the map. Always look for the directional sign first when studying a map.

If you were in Omaha, Nebraska, which way would you go to get to the cities listed below? Use a United States map from an atlas or encyclopedia to locate the cities. Be sure to check the directional sign so you know which way is north.

Write the direction you would travel to get from Omaha to each city listed. Use these abbreviations:

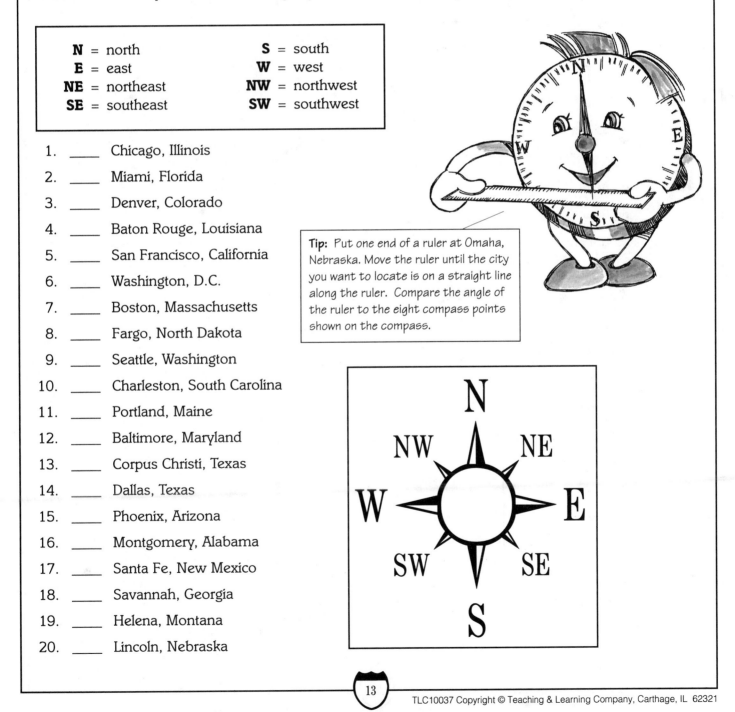

N = north   **S** = south
E = east   **W** = west
NE = northeast   **NW** = northwest
SE = southeast   **SW** = southwest

1. ____ Chicago, Illinois
2. ____ Miami, Florida
3. ____ Denver, Colorado
4. ____ Baton Rouge, Louisiana
5. ____ San Francisco, California
6. ____ Washington, D.C.
7. ____ Boston, Massachusetts
8. ____ Fargo, North Dakota
9. ____ Seattle, Washington
10. ____ Charleston, South Carolina
11. ____ Portland, Maine
12. ____ Baltimore, Maryland
13. ____ Corpus Christi, Texas
14. ____ Dallas, Texas
15. ____ Phoenix, Arizona
16. ____ Montgomery, Alabama
17. ____ Santa Fe, New Mexico
18. ____ Savannah, Georgia
19. ____ Helena, Montana
20. ____ Lincoln, Nebraska

Tip: Put one end of a ruler at Omaha, Nebraska. Move the ruler until the city you want to locate is on a straight line along the ruler. Compare the angle of the ruler to the eight compass points shown on the compass.

Which Way to El Dorado?

If you were in Little Rock, Arkansas, which way would you go to get to the cities listed below? Write the direction you would travel to get from Little Rock to each city listed. Use these abbreviations:

Arkansas has places named Airport, Bald Knob, Bloomer, Bullfrog Valley, Coal Hill, Coy, England, Grubbs, Huff, Rover, Success and Tulip.

N = north		**S** = south
E = east		**W** = west
NE = northeast		**NW** = northwest
SE = southeast		**SW** = southwest

1. ____ El Dorado
2. ____ Fort Smith
3. ____ Fayetteville
4. ____ Augusta
5. ____ Stuttgart
6. ____ Mountain Home
7. ____ Piggot
8. ____ Pocahontas
9. ____ Berryville
10. ____ Walnut Ridge
11. ____ Jonesboro
12. ____ Mariana
13. ____ Warren
14. ____ Arkadelphia
15. ____ Clinton
16. ____ Searcy
17. ____ Helena
18. ____ Salem
19. ____ Crossett
20. ____ Stamps

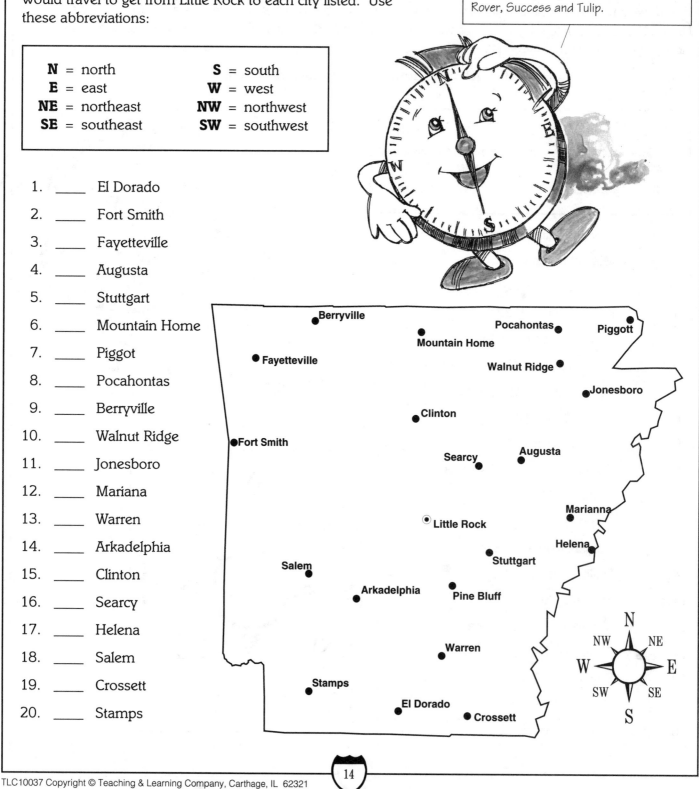

X Marks the Spot

Follow the directions below to discover the location of the mystery city. Use an Ohio state map from an atlas to find your way around the map below. Write the names of the cities shown in bold letters on the blanks on the map as you find them.

1. Starting in Columbus, Ohio, go south to **Circleville**.

2. From Circleville, go southwest to **Cincinnati**.

3. From Cincinnati, it's only a short hop north to **Dayton**.

4. Continue heading north to **Vandalia** and then to **Troy**.

5. Now go northeast to **Delaware** (the city, not the state).

6. From Delaware, head northeast again to **Akron**.

7. After a short stay in Akron, go south to **Marietta**, then west to **Athens**.

8. Now take a long trip northwest to **Bowling Green**.

9. You're almost to the end of your journey. Head south to **Bellefontaine**.

10. Finally, you're ready for the last stop. Head south to a city that begins with *X*. Make an *X* on the map to mark the spot.

    What is the name of the city you found? _____

Columbus

Ohio has cities and towns that begin with every letter of the alphabet—even J, Q, X and Z.

15

Pinpoint the State

To the Teacher

Object of this activity: Students use directional skills to pinpoint an unknown state.

Hang a large U.S. map on the bulletin board. Give students a copy of the U.S. map found at the back of this book.

Select one student to go first. Blindfold the student. Lead the blindfolded student to the bulletin board. Ask him to point to a spot anywhere on the map. Turn the student away from the map and remove the blindfold.

Ask the rest of the class to look at their maps and find the state the student pointed to when blindfolded.

The student who is "it" can look at the map on the bulletin board and ask questions to pinpoint the mystery state. Only questions that can be answered *yes* or *no* are allowed.

For example, the student might ask,

> "Is the state east of Arkansas."

> "Is the state south of Kansas?"

> "Does the name of the state begin with an *M*?"

When the student asks a question, have the rest of the class look at their maps of the U.S. and answer the question *yes* or *no*.

By asking a series of directional questions, the student can pinpoint the location of the state. When the student correctly guesses the state, he can select someone to go next.

You can also play this game with a large road map of a state. Instead of trying to guess the states, students would ask questions to pinpoint a specific city.

I'm Thinking of a Country

To play I'm Thinking of a Country display a large world map and/or a globe for students. Give students a clue about which country you're thinking of: "The country I'm thinking of is in Asia," or "The country I'm thinking of is in the Eastern Hemisphere," or "The country I'm thinking of borders on the Pacific Ocean."

Students take turns asking yes/no questions to determine the country.

The first student to correctly guess the country thinks of another country and gives a clue.

16

Finding Your Way Around a Map

A map **grid** is a system of imaginary lines that cross. These lines help locate places on a map.

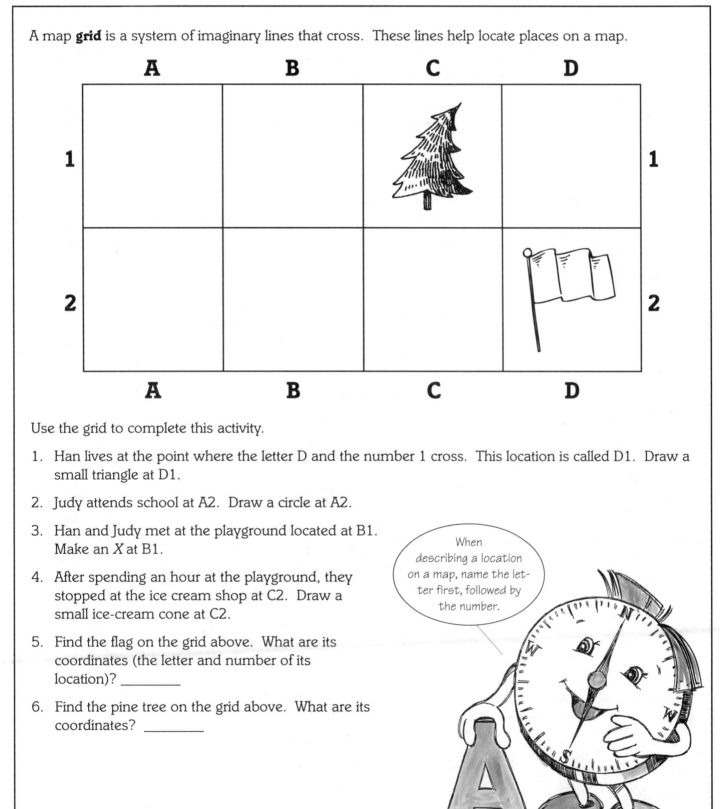

Use the grid to complete this activity.

1. Han lives at the point where the letter D and the number 1 cross. This location is called D1. Draw a small triangle at D1.

2. Judy attends school at A2. Draw a circle at A2.

3. Han and Judy met at the playground located at B1. Make an *X* at B1.

4. After spending an hour at the playground, they stopped at the ice cream shop at C2. Draw a small ice-cream cone at C2.

5. Find the flag on the grid above. What are its coordinates (the letter and number of its location)? _____

6. Find the pine tree on the grid above. What are its coordinates? _____

When describing a location on a map, name the letter first, followed by the number.

Name _____

Zap! You're in North Dakota

Look at the map of North Dakota. Notice the letters across the top of the map and the numbers along the side. Use the letters and numbers to name the coordinates of the cities listed below. If a city is partway between letters or numbers, use the closest one.

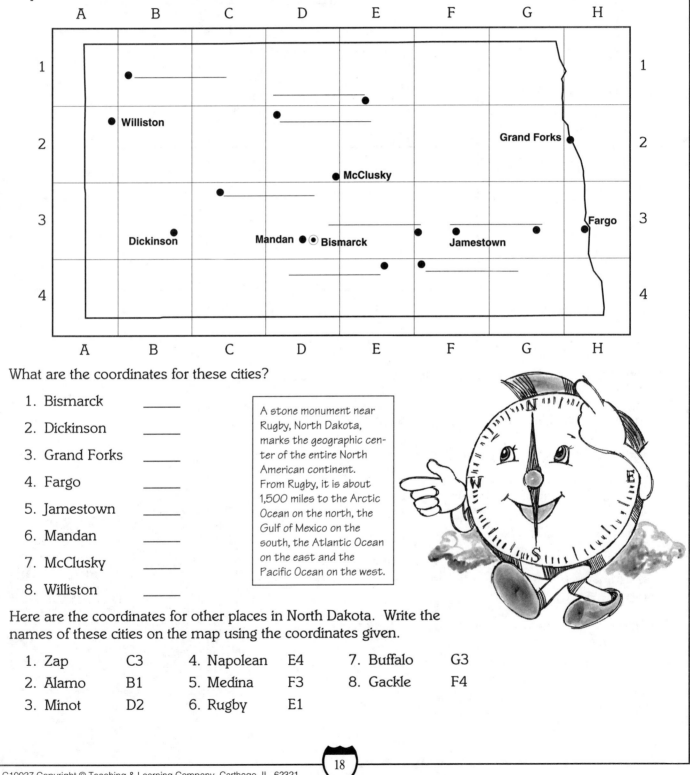

What are the coordinates for these cities?

1. Bismarck _____
2. Dickinson _____
3. Grand Forks _____
4. Fargo _____
5. Jamestown _____
6. Mandan _____
7. McClusky _____
8. Williston _____

A stone monument near Rugby, North Dakota, marks the geographic center of the entire North American continent. From Rugby, it is about 1,500 miles to the Arctic Ocean on the north, the Gulf of Mexico on the south, the Atlantic Ocean on the east and the Pacific Ocean on the west.

Here are the coordinates for other places in North Dakota. Write the names of these cities on the map using the coordinates given.

1. Zap	C3	4. Napolean	E4	7. Buffalo	G3
2. Alamo	B1	5. Medina	F3	8. Gackle	F4
3. Minot	D2	6. Rugby	E1		

18

Grid Work

A grid helps locate specific places on a map. To solve this puzzle, find the letter in the grid that matches the coordinates (letter and number) below each blank. For example: C1 on the grid would represent the letter *K*.

	1	**2**	**3**	**4**	**5**	
A	A	B	C	D	E	**A**
B	F	G	H	I	J	**B**
C	K	L	M	N	O	**C**
D	P	R	S	T	U	**D**
E	V	W	X	Y	Z	**E**
	1	**2**	**3**	**4**	**5**	

1. __ __ __ __ __
   A2 C5 B4 D3 A5

2. __ __ __ __ __
   D3 A1 C2 A5 C3

3. __ __ __ __ __ __
   B3 A5 C2 A5 C4 A1

4. __ __ __ __ __ __
   B5 D5 C4 A5 A1 D5

5. __ __ __ __ __ __
   A2 C5 D3 D4 C5 C4

6. __ __ __ __ __ __
   A1 D5 D3 D4 B4 C4

7. __ __ __ __ __ __
   D4 C5 D1 A5 C1 A1

8. __ __ __ __ __ __
   D1 B4 A5 D2 D2 A5

9. __ __ __ __ __ __
   A1 C2 A2 A1 C4 E4

10. __ __ __ __ __ __ __
    A1 D5 B2 D5 D3 D4 A1

11. __ __ __ __ __ __ __
    C5 C2 E4 C3 D1 B4 A1

12. __ __ __ __ __ __ __
    D1 B3 C5 A5 C4 B4 E3

13. __ __ __ __ __ __ __
    C3 A1 A4 B4 D3 C5 C4

14. __ __ __ __ __ __ __
    A1 D4 C2 A1 C4 D4 A1

15. __ __ __ __ __ __ __
    C2 B4 C4 A3 C5 C2 C4

16. __ __ __ __ __ __ __
    C2 A1 C4 D3 B4 C4 B2

17. __ __ __ __ __ __ __ __
    A2 B4 D3 C3 A1 D2 A3 C1

18. __ __ __ __ __ __ __ __
    B3 C5 C4 C5 C2 D5 C2 D5

19. __ __ __ __ __ __ __ __
    D2 B4 A3 B3 C3 C5 C4 A4

20. __ __ __ __ __ __ __ __
    A3 C5 C2 D5 C3 A2 B4 A1

21. __ __ __ __ __ __ __ __
    A3 B3 A5 E4 A5 C4 C4 A5

22. __ __ __ __ __ __ __ __ __ __
    D3 A1 A3 D2 A1 C3 A5 C4 D4 C5

Write the name of your city, using the letters and numbers from the grid: __ __ __ __ __ __ __ __ __ __ __ __ __ __ __

The Equator and Other Imaginary Lines

The **equator** is an imaginary line that goes around the middle of the Earth at its widest point. It divides the Earth into two sections: the Northern Hemisphere and the Southern Hemisphere.

Look at a globe. Find the equator. Name three countries at or near the equator.

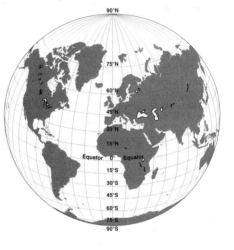

_____   _____   _____

Name three countries in the Northern Hemisphere.

_____   _____   _____

Name three countries in the Southern Hemisphere.

_____   _____   _____

Globes and world maps usually show imaginary lines called latitude and longitude. Lines of **latitude** run parallel to the equator and to each other. **Parallels** is another word for lines of latitude.

A globe is divided into 360 degrees, like a circle. Lines of latitude measure the distance north or south of the equator in degrees. The equator has a latitude of zero degrees. The North and South Poles have a latitude of 90 degrees.

1. Draw a straight line across the circle at its widest point. Label it EQUATOR.

2. Draw two lines parallel to the equator across the top half of the circle to divide it into three equal parts.

Hemi means "half." Sphere means "a round object." Hemisphere means "one-half of a round object" like a globe.

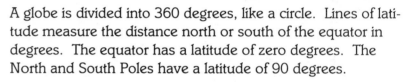

3. The line you drew above the equator is called the TROPIC OF CANCER. Label it on the circle. It is 23½ degrees north of the equator.

4. The top line you drew is called the ARCTIC CIRCLE. Label it.

5. Divide the bottom half of the circle into three equal parts.

6. Label the TROPIC OF CAPRICORN—the line closest to the equator. It is 23½ degrees south of the equator.

7. Label the bottom line ANTARCTIC CIRCLE.

20

More Imaginary Lines

Besides lines of latitude, globes and world maps contain another set of imaginary lines. Lines of **longitude** run from the North Pole to the South Pole. Another name for lines of longitude is **meridians**.

One line of longitude, called the **prime meridian** passes through Greenwich, England. The prime meridian is the longest line of latitude. It divides the Earth into the Eastern Hemisphere and the Western Hemisphere. Greenwich is zero degrees longitude. There are 180 degrees of longitude west of Greenwich and 180 degrees east of Greenwich. The symbol for degrees is °.

Find the prime meridian on a globe. Name three countries at or near the prime meridian.

_____   _____   _____

Name three countries in the Eastern Hemisphere.

_____   _____   _____

Name three countries in the Western Hemisphere.

_____   _____   _____

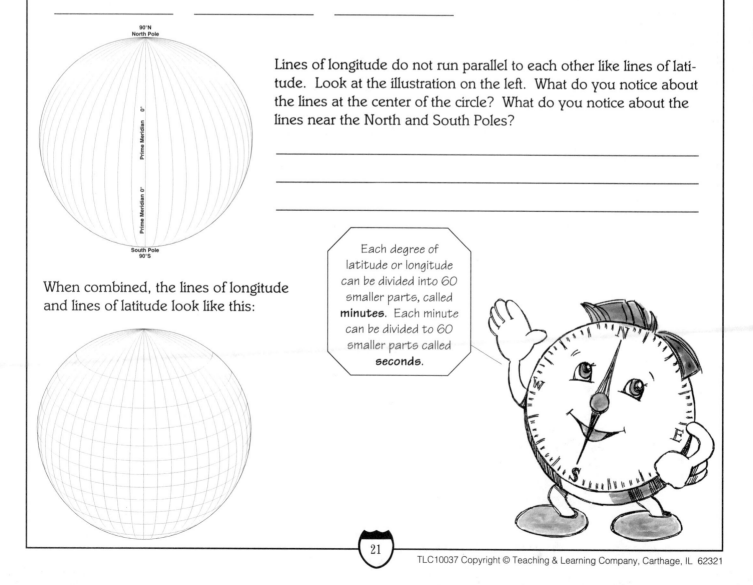

Lines of longitude do not run parallel to each other like lines of latitude. Look at the illustration on the left. What do you notice about the lines at the center of the circle? What do you notice about the lines near the North and South Poles?

_____

_____

_____

When combined, the lines of longitude and lines of latitude look like this:

Each degree of latitude or longitude can be divided into 60 smaller parts, called **minutes**. Each minute can be divided to 60 smaller parts called **seconds**.

On a Flat Map

Lines of latitude and longitude can also be found on most world maps. Like a letter and number grid, these lines help locate places on a map.

Discussion Topic

Compare the way lines of latitude and longitude look on a flat map and on a globe. How are they different? Why do you think they look different?

Look at a world map in an atlas. Find the equator. Locate the line of latitude marked 20° North that runs through Africa, India and Mexico. Remember lines of latitude run parallel to the equator.

1. What are four countries crossed by the line marked 20° South? _____ _____
   _____ _____

2. What line of latitude runs across the middle of the continental United States? _____
   (Be sure to specify North or South.)

Find the prime meridian. Locate the line of longitude marked 20° East that crosses through Sweden, Poland and cuts Africa almost in half. Remember, lines of longitude cross the equator.

3. What are two countries crossed by the line of longitude marked 20° West? _____ and
   _____

4. What line of longitude runs through the middle of the United States? _____ (Be sure to
   specify East or West.)

5. The big island of Hawaii is along which line of latitude? _____ (Be sure to
   specify North or South.)

Select three countries and write their names below. Show what lines of latitude and longitude meet in each country.

Country	**Line of latitude**	**Line of longitude**
_____	_____	_____
_____	_____	_____
_____	_____	_____

When naming a line of latitude, always give the direction North or South so people know if it is North or South of the Equator. Lines of longitude need to be labeled East or West to show which direction they are from the Prime Meridian.

22

Pinpointing Places

Lines of latitude and longitude can pinpoint any place on Earth very precisely. Each degree of latitude or longitude can be divided into 60 smaller parts called **minutes**. Each minute can be divided into 60 smaller parts called **seconds**.

The symbol ° is used for degrees. Minutes are shown with a ' sign and seconds with this symbol: ".

Written out, a place that is 32 degrees, 27 minutes and 5 seconds North latitude and 99 degrees, 43 minutes and 51 seconds West longitude would look like this: 32° 27' 05" N, 99° 43' 51" W

If you looked on a map, you would find that 32° 27' 05" N, 99° 43' 51" W pinpoints Abilene, Texas.

Most people do not need to pinpoint places that precisely. You can use only degrees and round those off to the nearest 10 for this activity.

Use a copy of the U.S. map at the back of this book to pinpoint the cities listed below. Write the name of the city in the correct location on the map.

City	Latitude North	Longitude West
Akron, OH	41	81
Atlanta, GA	33	84
Baltimore, MD	39	76
Berkeley, CA	37	122
Butte, MT	46	112
Charleston, WV	38	81
Dallas, TX	32	96
Fairbanks, AK	64	147
Miami, FL	25	80
Portland, OR	45	122
Pueblo, CO	38	104
Wichita, KS	37	97

Discussion Topics

Do cities in the northern part of the U.S. have a higher or lower degree of North latitude than cities in the southern part? Why?

Do cities on the East Coast have a higher or lower degree of West latitude than cities on the West Coast? Why?

Finding Places Around the World

Review: **Latitude** is measured in degrees, minutes and seconds. Lines of latitude measure the distance north or south of the equator. The equator has a latitude of zero degrees. The North and South Poles have a latitude of 90 degrees. Lines of latitude run parallel to the equator and to each other.

Longitude is also measured in degrees, minutes and seconds. Lines of **longitude** run from the North Pole to the South Pole. The **prime meridian** passes through Greenwich, England, and is zero degrees longitude. There are 180 degrees of longitude west of Greenwich and 180 degrees east of Greenwich.

Use a copy of the world map at the back of this book for this activity. Write the name of the cities listed in the correct locations on the map. For this activity, you can round the degrees of latitude and longitude to the nearest 10.

City	Latitude	Longitude	City	Latitude	Longitude
Athens, Greece	37 N	23 E	Mecca, Saudi Arabia	21 N	39 E
Bangkok, Thailand	13 N	100 E	Mexico City, Mexico	19 N	99 W
Beijing, China	39 N	116 E	Moscow, Russia	55 N	37 E
Berlin, Germany	52 N	13 E	Panama City, Panama	08 N	79 W
Bombay, India	18 N	72 E	Rome, Italy	41 N	12 E
Cairo, Egypt	30 N	31 E	Santiago, Chile	33 S	70 W
Hilo, Hawaii, USA	19 N	155 W	St. Johns, Nfld., Canada	47 N	52 W
Jakarta, Indonesia	06 S	106 E	Sydney, Australia	33 S	151 E
Jerusalem, Israel	31 N	35 E	Tokyo, Japan	35 S	139 E
London, England	51 N	00	Wellington, New Zealand	41 S	174 E

Discussion Topic

The North Pole and the South Pole do not have lines of longitude. Why not?

Only one place on Earth could have 00 latitude and 00 longitude. Why? Where would that place be?

What Time Is It?

Lines of longitude are used to mark **time zones** around the world. At the Equator, the Earth is divided into 24 parts. Each time zone is 15 degrees wide, the approximate distance the Sun travels in one hour.

Look at a globe or world map. Starting at the Prime Meridian (0° longitude) which passes through Greenwich, England, time changes with each 15 degrees of longitude. East of Greenwich, the time is ahead (later). West of Greenwich, the time is behind (earlier).

Places may share the same time zone even if they are far apart like New York City and Lima, Peru, as long as they lie within the same lines of longitude.

A **time zone map** tells you the time in different parts of the world. There are four time zones in the continental U.S.—Pacific, Mountain, Central and Eastern. Alaska and Hawaii are in different time zones.

Use the time zone map of the continental United States on the next page to answer these questions:

1. When it is 9 A.M. in Maine, what time is it in New Mexico? _____

2. When it is 2 P.M. in Corpus Christi, Texas, what time is it in California? _____

3. When it is 6 A.M. in Portland, Oregon, what time is it in Orlando, Florida? _____

4. When it is 3 P.M. in Michigan, what time is it in Nevada? _____

5. What is the western most time zone in the continental U.S. called? _____

6. What time zone is east of the central time zone? _____

7. Alaska is west of the pacific time zone. When it is 5 P.M. in the pacific time zone, do you think it 4 P.M. or 6 P.M. in Alaska? Why?_____

    _____

8. In Hawaii it is two hours earlier than pacific time. When it is 8 P.M. eastern time, what time would it be in Hawaii? _____

9. What time zone do you live in? _____

Discussion Topic

Why do you think the Earth is divided into 24 time zones?

Time Zones Across the United States

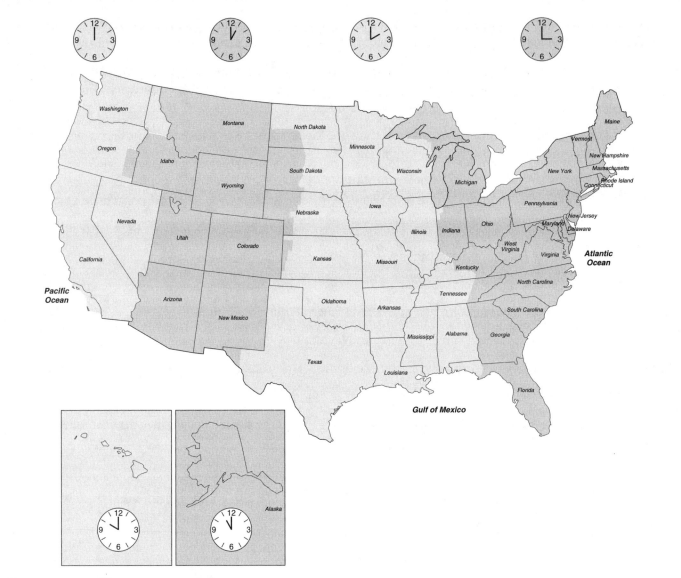

Discussion Topics

Have a globe or world map showing time zones available for reference.

Compare this map to a map showing lines of longitude. Do the time zone lines exactly follow lines of longitude? Why not?

Illinois and Indiana are next to each other but are in different time zones. Why?

Minnesota and Texas are far away from each other but are in the same time zones. Why?

New York City and Lima, Peru, are in the same time zone. New York City and Chicago are in different time zones, even though the cities are much closer to each other. Why?

Why is it important to know what time it is in different parts of the world?

26

How Far?

It would be impossible to draw everything on most maps in actual size. How would you ever fold a map the size of Texas? Maps are miniature versions of real places.

Because maps come in all sizes, we need to know how much area the map represents. A map scale tells us the actual distance between places compared to the distance shown on the map.

If 1 inch equals 100 miles on a map, 3 inches equals 300 miles, 5 inches equals 500 miles and 7½ inches equals 750 miles.

A. If one inch equal 25 miles, how many miles does 6 inches equal? _____

B. If one inch equals 1,000 miles how many miles does ½ inch equal? _____

C. If one inch equals 7 miles, how many inches equals 21 miles? _____

D. If one inch equals 100 miles, how many inches equals 75 miles? _____

Look at the map below and the two maps on the next page. Although Alaska is nearly 500 times larger than Rhode Island, and the continental U.S. is much larger than Alaska, all three maps are about the same size.

Cities in Rhode Island that are one inch away are much closer in reality than cities one inch apart on the Alaska map. The scale below each map helps you determine distance.

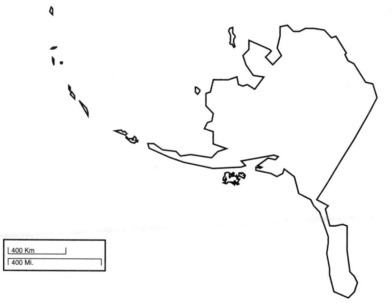

| 400 Km |
| 400 Mi. |

1. _____ One inch equals how many miles on the Alaska map?

2. _____ How far could you travel in a straight line from east to west across Alaska?

3. _____ How far could you travel in a straight line across Alaska from north to south at the longest point?

How Far?

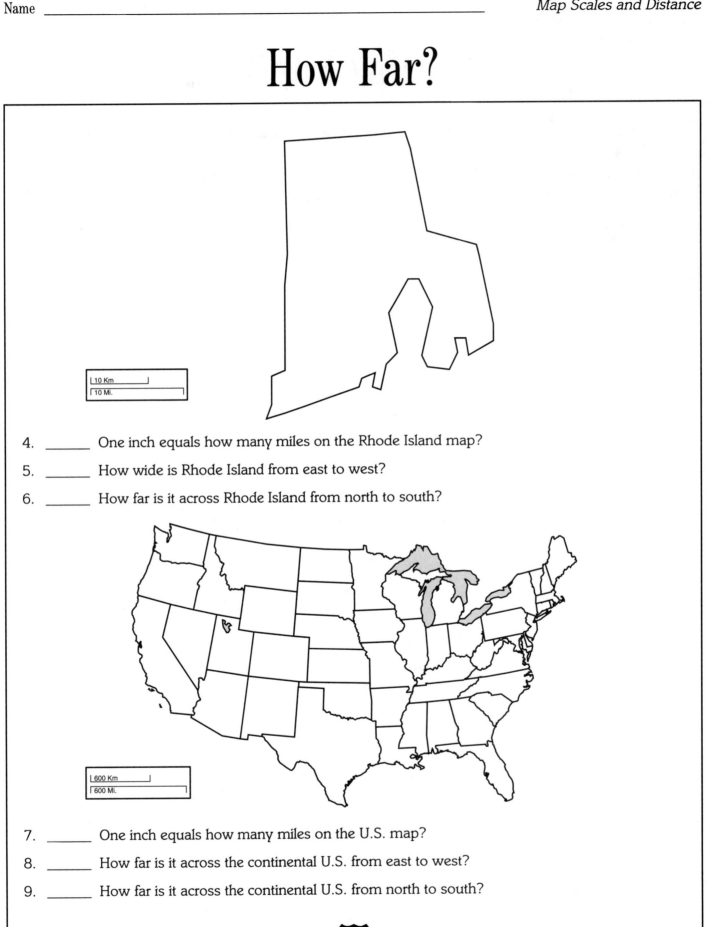

| 10 Km |
| 10 Mi. |

4. _____ One inch equals how many miles on the Rhode Island map?

5. _____ How wide is Rhode Island from east to west?

6. _____ How far is it across Rhode Island from north to south?

| 600 Km |
| 600 Mi. |

7. _____ One inch equals how many miles on the U.S. map?

8. _____ How far is it across the continental U.S. from east to west?

9. _____ How far is it across the continental U.S. from north to south?

Drawing a Map to Scale

A floor plan is a map of a room, drawn to scale. Select a room in your home or school. Measure the length and width of the room with a tape measure. Write the dimensions here:

width = _____ feet; length = _____ feet

Once you know how large the room is, decide on the scale. The scale depends on the size of the room and the size of the paper you use. If the room is fairly small, you may decide one inch on your map equals one foot. If the room is too large to fit using that scale, you may decide one inch equals two, three or four feet.

Fill in the information for the scale you will use.

$$\left[\frac{}{\text{one inch}} \right] = \underline{} \text{ feet}$$

Draw your room. Add details like the location of furniture, doors and windows, also drawn to scale.

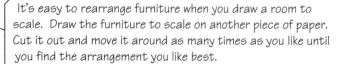

It's easy to rearrange furniture when you draw a room to scale. Draw the furniture to scale on another piece of paper. Cut it out and move it around as many times as you like until you find the arrangement you like best.

As the Crow Flies

Use the map scale and a ruler to determine how far you would travel in a straight line to get from one city to another in Texas. Write your answer in approximate number of miles.

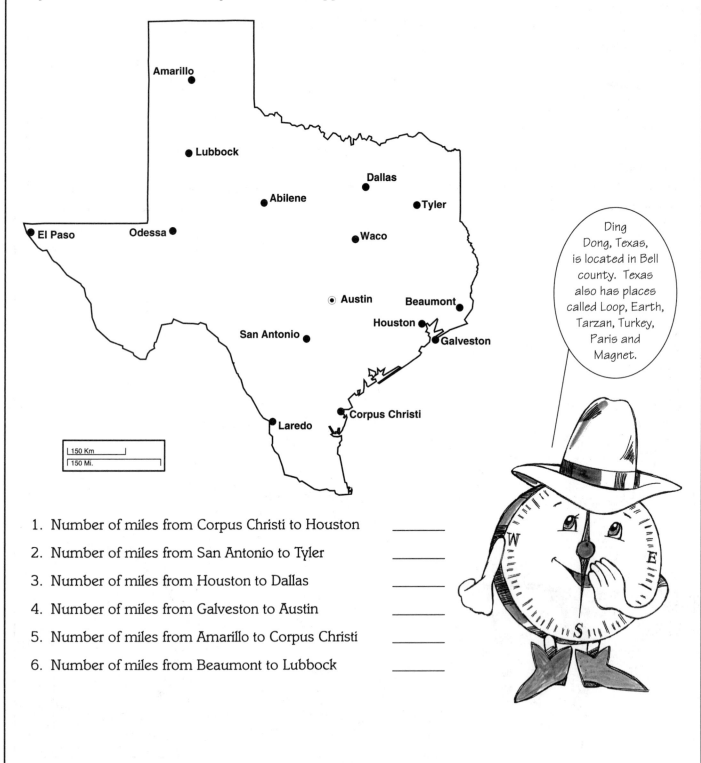

1. Number of miles from Corpus Christi to Houston   _____
2. Number of miles from San Antonio to Tyler   _____
3. Number of miles from Houston to Dallas   _____
4. Number of miles from Galveston to Austin   _____
5. Number of miles from Amarillo to Corpus Christi   _____
6. Number of miles from Beaumont to Lubbock   _____

30

Name _____   *Direction and Distance*

Colorado Vacation

It's time for a Colorado vacation. When your plane landed at the Denver airport, you discovered a problem. Someone forgot to fill in the information on the signs below, so you'll have to do it yourself.

Find the places on the Colorado map. Use the map scale, map compass and a ruler. Fill in the distance and direction you would go from Denver to get to each place. Use the abbreviations N,S,E,W, NE, NW, SE and SW.

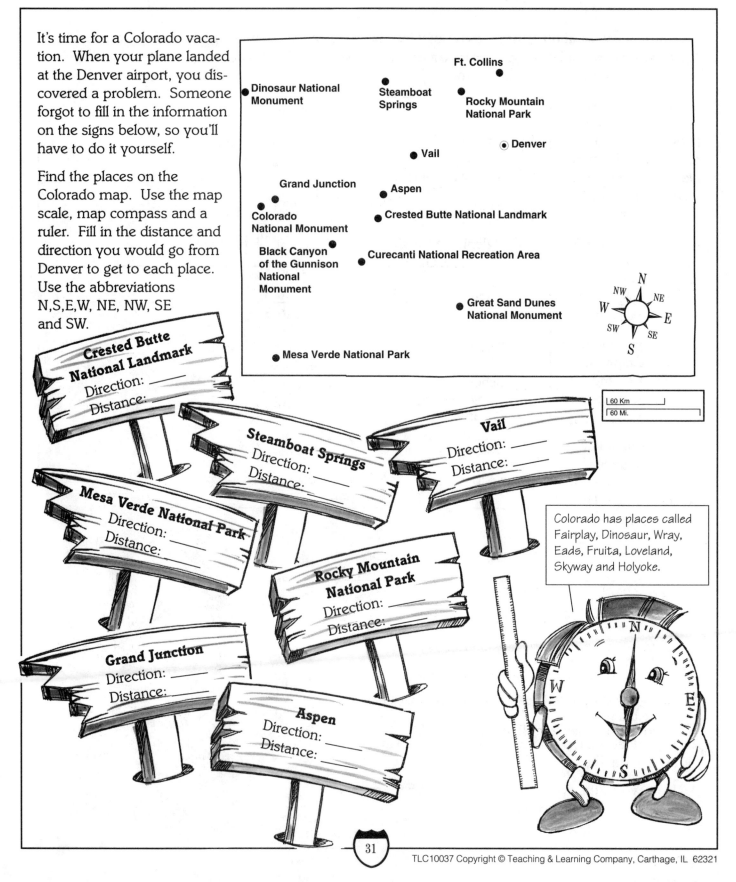

Crested Butte National Landmark
Direction: _____
Distance: _____

Steamboat Springs
Direction: _____
Distance: _____

Vail
Direction: _____
Distance: _____

Mesa Verde National Park
Direction: _____
Distance: _____

Rocky Mountain National Park
Direction: _____
Distance: _____

Grand Junction
Direction: _____
Distance: _____

Aspen
Direction: _____
Distance: _____

Colorado has places called Fairplay, Dinosaur, Wray, Eads, Fruita, Loveland, Skyway and Holyoke.

Map labels: Ft. Collins, Dinosaur National Monument, Steamboat Springs, Rocky Mountain National Park, Denver, Vail, Grand Junction, Aspen, Colorado National Monument, Crested Butte National Landmark, Black Canyon of the Gunnison National Monument, Curecanti National Recreation Area, Great Sand Dunes National Monument, Mesa Verde National Park. Scale: 60 Km, 60 Mi.

31

TLC10037 Copyright © Teaching & Learning Company, Carthage, IL 62321

Map Symbols: What Do They Mean?

Mapmakers use **symbols** (small pictures of things that are real) to show where objects can be found. Most maps contain a box called a **map key** or **legend**. This is the key to understanding what symbols are used on the map and what they mean.

Mapmakers try to use symbols that remind people of the item represented. For example, a picture of an airplane could mark the location of an airport.

Map symbols should be simple pictures. Here are some symbols that might be used on a city map.

Your Turn: In the map key to the right, draw symbols to stand for each of the items listed.

Study the map keys of several different kinds of maps. How are the symbols alike? How are they different?

Map Key

✈ Airport	⛺ Campground
🏛 Government Building	⛳ Public Golf Course
🚢 Harbor	🛝 Playground
☎ Telephone Booth	🧯 Fire Station

Map Key

Post Office	Hospital
School	Railroad Tracks
Library	River
Swimming Pool	Zoo
Mall	Nature Trail

When I see a map key, I always look for the symbol for the pizza places.

_____

_____

_____

Discussion Questions

1. Why do different maps use different symbols for the same things?

2. How does the type of map determine what kinds of symbols are used?

3. How would the symbols on a city map differ from the symbols used on a world map?

32

Getting Around the Mall

Most malls provide a map so people can find their way around. A map key could be used to show where each type of store or other facility is located. Draw symbols in the map key for these places in a mall:

Map Key

Music 9, 25	Shoe Store 5, 15
Pet Store 30	Restaurant 21, 28, 32, 33
Jewelry 3, 12, 23	Candy and Nut Shop 22
Grocery Store 13	Bookstore 27, 31
Hardware 1, 18	Video Arcade 11
Sporting Goods 2, 16	Appliances 24, 26
Computer 7, 14	Rest Rooms 19, 35
Gift Shop 6, 8, 17	Telephone 20, 34
Clothing 4, 10	Information Center 29

Each type of place in the map key is numbered to match its location(s) on the mall map below. Draw the correct symbol on the mall map to show what type each place is. For example, if you used a picture of a telephone in the map key, draw a telephone in numbers 20 and 34.

TLC10037 Copyright © Teaching & Learning Company, Carthage, IL 62321

Africa

One type of information usually found in a map key is the symbol used for the capital of a state or country. Most maps indicate the capitals with some type of a star. On the map of Africa on the next page, capital cities are marked with a ★. The location of other cities is marked with a ●.

Africa is one of the seven continents and includes many countries. Study the map of Africa. Find the capital cities of the countries listed and write them on the blanks.

Country	Capital	Country	Capital
1. Algeria	_____	8. Liberia	_____
2. Angola	_____	9. Mali	_____
3. Botswana	_____	10. Niger	_____
4. Chad	_____	11. Sierra Leone	_____
5. Egypt	_____	12. Somalia	_____
6. Ethiopia	_____	13. Uganda	_____
7. Kenya	_____	14. Zaire	_____

Use the directional indicator on the map to answer the questions.

15. Is Libya east or west of Egypt? _____

16. Which ocean forms the western boundary of Africa? _____

17. Is Tanzania north or south of the equator? _____

18. What is the name of the large island along the east coast of Africa? _____

19. What sea forms the northern boundary of Africa? _____

20. The equator runs through what six countries in Africa?

_____   _____

_____   _____

_____

_____

> Lesotho is a small country completely surrounded by a larger one, South Africa.

Did You Know?

The country of South Africa has three capitals. Cape Town is the Legislative capital, Pretoria is the Administrative capital and Bloemfontein is the Judicial capital.

The Continent of Africa Map

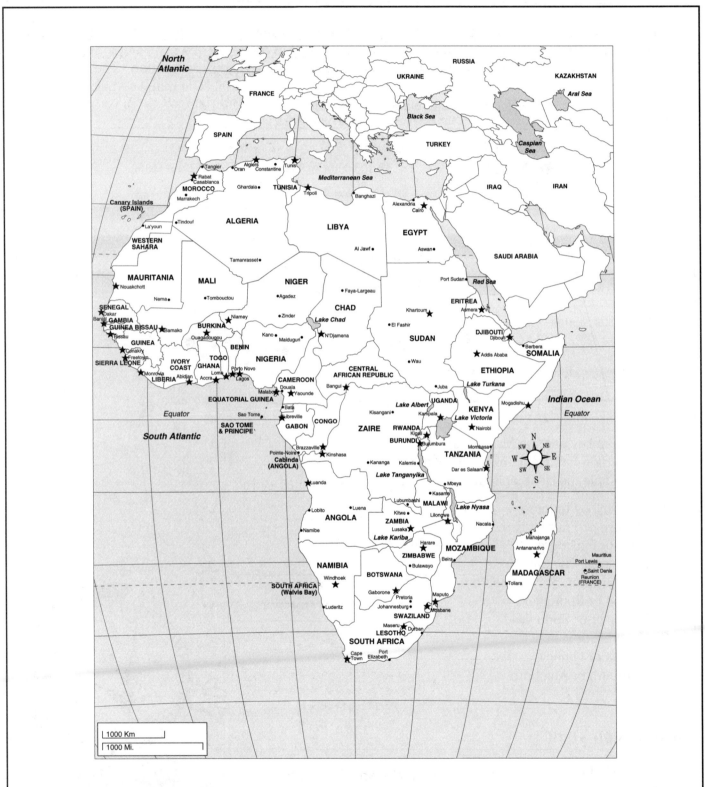

City Size

When you look at a map, how can you tell if a city is large or small? Is it a large metropolitan area or a small village? One way is to look at the size of the print used to name the city. The larger the letters, the larger the city. Another way is to look at the size of the dot that marks the location. The smaller the dot, the smaller the city. Map keys often contain this type of information. The map key below uses both type size and dot size to show the relative size of cities in Massachusetts.

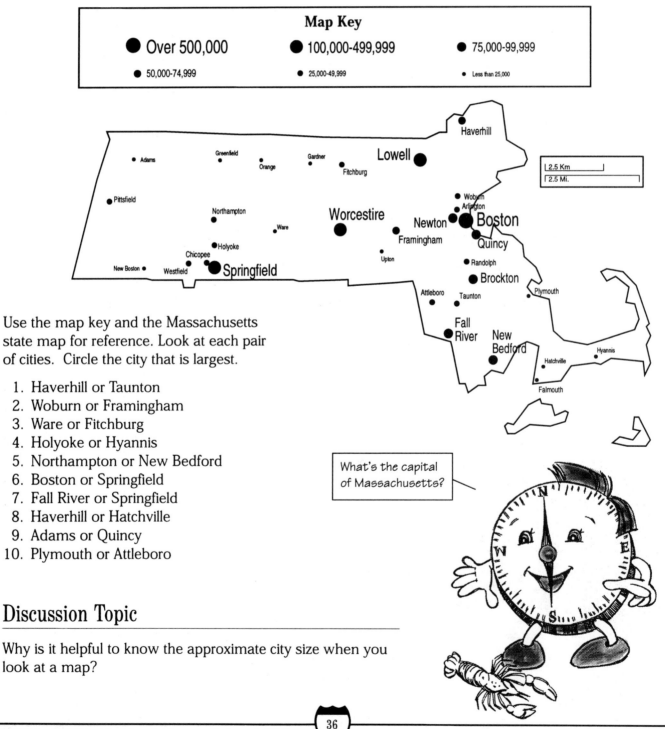

Use the map key and the Massachusetts state map for reference. Look at each pair of cities. Circle the city that is largest.

1. Haverhill or Taunton
2. Woburn or Framingham
3. Ware or Fitchburg
4. Holyoke or Hyannis
5. Northampton or New Bedford
6. Boston or Springfield
7. Fall River or Springfield
8. Haverhill or Hatchville
9. Adams or Quincy
10. Plymouth or Attleboro

Discussion Topic

_____

Why is it helpful to know the approximate city size when you look at a map?

A Map of Somewhere Else

Maps can be of real places or imaginary ones. J.R.R. Tolkien, author of *The Hobbit*, drew a map of Middle Earth, the home of hobbits, wizards, elves, trolls, dwarfs and dragons.

What book have you read that shows a map of an imaginary place?

_____

Draw your own map of an imaginary place. You could make a map for a place you've read about, like Dorothy's journey in *The Wizard of Oz*. You could draw a map of a place you made up yourself and write a short story to go with the map. Add as much detail as you can. Label your map and all important places on the map. Be sure to include a scale, a map key and a compass.

I'd like to visit the planet Pern. Perhaps Anne McCaffrey would send me a map if I wrote her a letter.

Let's Visit Yellowstone National Park

Would you like to watch Old Faithful blow its top or hear the slurping and burping of mud pots in Yellowstone National Park? With so many spectacular geysers, hot springs and other fantastic sites, we'll need a detailed map so we won't miss anything.

Use the partial map of Yellowstone National Park on the next page to complete this activity.

1. Let's start our tour of Yellowstone at Old Faithful, the most popular site in the park. Circle Old Faithful on the map.

2. As we head north to see the Great Fountain Geyser, we'll pass by four "Basins." What are they called? _____ _____ _____ _____

3. You'll want to get out of the car and take a short walk to see Great Fountain Geyser. Trace the route of the Three Senses Trail in red.

4. As we continue north to Madison, the road follows along a river. What is the river called? _____

5. Two areas along the way are marked with this symbol: π What does this symbol mean? _____

6. How far is it from Madison to Old Faithful? _____

7. After watching Steamboat Geyser, we'll continue on to Norris. Are there camping facilities at Norris? _____

8. It might be fun to tour some of the park on bicycle. Follow the road east from Norris. What is the next town? _____

9. Back on the bicycle, we'll head south from Canyon Village. Would you like to see a majestic waterfall? What is the name of the first waterfall you will find? _____

10. South again to Sulphur Cauldron and a stop at the Mud Volcano. Circle these two sites on the map, then continue south.

11. What lake is south of the Fishing Bridge? _____

12. Where is the nearest campsite on the west shore of the lake?

_____

13. If we take the bicycle tour near Bridge Bay, what will we see?

_____

14. We'll end our tour at a village on the southwest shore of West Thumb. What is the village called?

_____

Yellowstone National Park Map

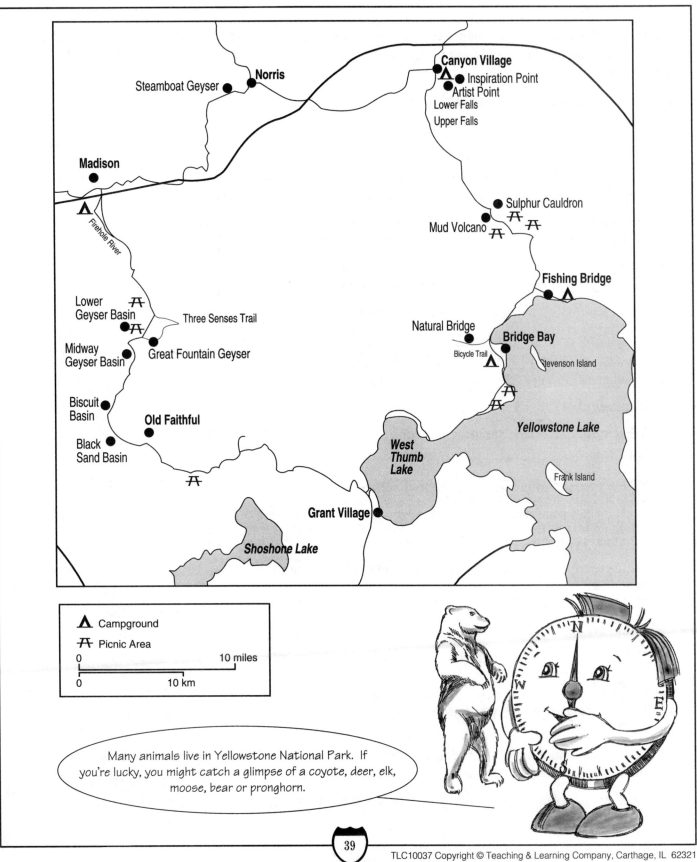

Canyon Village

Inspiration Point

Artist Point

Lower Falls

Upper Falls

Steamboat Geyser

Norris

Madison

Firehole River

Sulphur Cauldron

Mud Volcano

Fishing Bridge

Lower Geyser Basin

Three Senses Trail

Natural Bridge

Bridge Bay

Midway Geyser Basin

Great Fountain Geyser

Bicycle Trail

Stevenson Island

Biscuit Basin

Old Faithful

Yellowstone Lake

Black Sand Basin

West Thumb Lake

Frank Island

Grant Village

Shoshone Lake

Λ Campground

丌 Picnic Area

0   10 miles

0   10 km

Many animals live in Yellowstone National Park. If you're lucky, you might catch a glimpse of a coyote, deer, elk, moose, bear or pronghorn.

Name _____

Road Maps

Road maps show roads in a given area. The map key on state road maps shows the type of roads, such as toll roads, interstate highways, U.S. highways, county roads and unpaved roads and other useful information.

Look at the map key for the Utah road map:

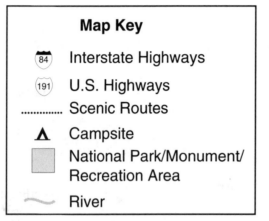

1. What symbol is used for interstate highways? _____

2. What symbol is used for state highways? _____

3. What symbol is used for scenic routes? _____

4. What symbol is used for campsites? _____

What other types of information does the map key show?

Look at the Utah state road map on the next page to answer these questions:

5. What interstate highway would you take to get from Cedar City to Provo? _____

6. Which road would you take to go from Heber City to Duchesne? _____ What type of road is it? _____

7. What symbol is used to indicate rivers? _____ Name two rivers that can be found on this Utah state map. _____ _____

8. Circle three campsites in green on the map.

9. What symbol is used to indicate a national park, monument or recreation area? _____

10. Which highways would you take to get from Flaming Gorge National Recreation Area to Dinosaur National Monument? _____

11. Arches National Park is a wonderful place to mountain bike. Which highways would you take to get from Salt Lake City to Arches National Park?_____

12. How many miles is it from Salt Lake City to Green River? _____

Traveling Through Utah

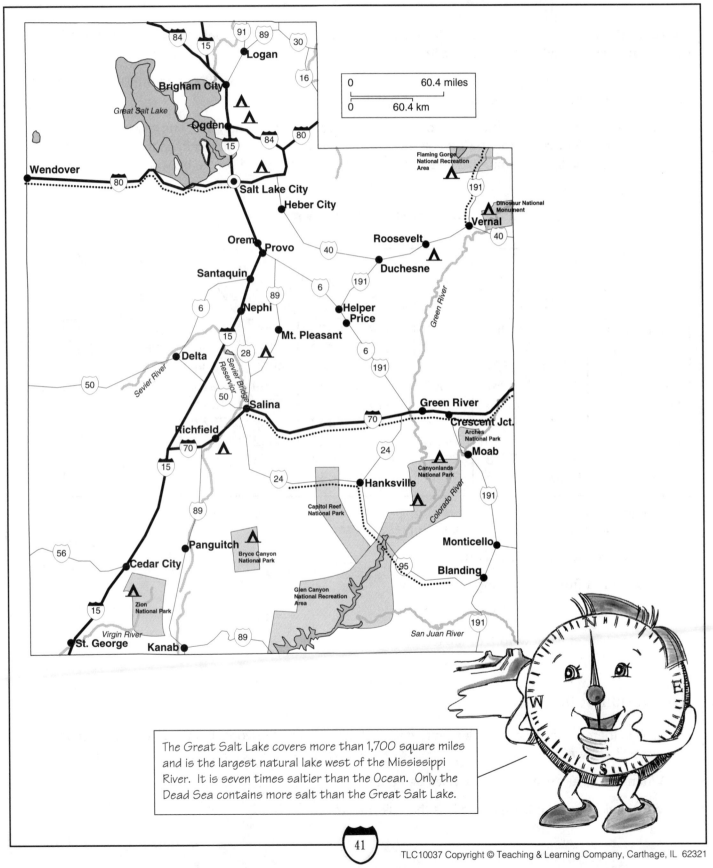

The Great Salt Lake covers more than 1,700 square miles and is the largest natural lake west of the Mississippi River. It is seven times saltier than the Ocean. Only the Dead Sea contains more salt than the Great Salt Lake.

Reading Mileage Charts

Mileage charts show how far apart cities are from each other. Mileage charts may show air distance between cities or road distance (distance by road).

On an air distance chart, you will find that New Orleans is 966 miles from Washington, D.C. On a road distance chart, the two cities are 1,085 miles apart.

To find the distance between two cities on a mileage chart, locate the name of one city along the top row. Find the other city along the left column. Draw an imaginary line down from the top and another one over from the left. The number where the two lines meet is the distance between the two cities.

Air Distances Between World Cities

	Buenos Aires	Hong Kong	Honolulu	London	Moscow	New York	Paris	Rome	Tokyo
Buenos Aires		11463	7558	6918	8375	5297	6877	6929	11400
Hong Kong	11463		5537	5981	4439	8051	5956	5768	1796
Honolulu	7558	5537		7226	7033	4959	7434	8022	3850
London	6918	5981	7226		1549	3459	213	887	5938
Moscow	8375	4439	7033	1549		4662	1541	1474	4650
New York	5297	8051	4959	3459	4662		3622	4273	6735
Paris	6877	5956	7434	213	1541	3622		682	6033
Rome	6929	5768	8022	887	1474	4273	682		6124
Tokyo	11400	1796	3850	5938	4650	6735	6033	6124	

Use the air distance chart above to answer these questions:

1. How far is it from Tokyo to London? _____

2. How far is it from Hong Kong to Honolulu? _____

3. How far is it from Paris to Rome? _____

4. Is Tokyo closer to New York or Moscow? _____

Discussion Topics

1. Why is there a difference in miles on these two types of charts? Does that mean one of the charts is wrong? Why not?

2. When would air miles and road miles be equal?

3. Why couldn't road miles ever be less than air miles?

Political Maps

Political maps show the **boundaries** of political units like countries, states or cities. A boundary is usually an invisible line which people have agreed to use. Boundaries between countries are also called **borders**. Some political maps use color to make places and boundaries easier to find.

Some boundaries are natural, physical ones. The Mississippi River is the boundary between Illinois and Iowa. Lake Ontario is part of the boundary between the United States and Canada.

What other kinds of natural boundaries can separate political units?

_____

A fence and a road are types of boundaries made by people. The Great Wall of China was built to defend the boundaries of that country in ancient times. What are some other examples of people-made boundaries?

_____

A map of the United States showing the boundaries of the states is a political map. Give three other examples of political maps.

_____

If you could divide the continental U.S. into states, how many states would you create? Why?

_____

_____

Would all the states be the same size? Why or why not? _____

_____

How would you decide on the state boundaries? _____

_____

Discussion Topics

1. Why do boundaries exist between countries?

2. What if there were no political boundaries?

3. How do you think people decide on boundaries?

4. Sometimes boundaries change? Why?

The border between the United States and Mexico is crossed by more people every year than any other boundary between two countries.

Switzerland, Indiana?

A state map showing counties is one type of **political map**. Texas has the most counties (254) and Delaware has the least (3). In Louisiana, the 64 counties are called parishes. Alaska is divided into 23 boroughs.

Study the county map of Indiana and answer the questions below.

1. Which county is in the most southwestern corner of Indiana? _____

2. What county is directly north of Montgomery county? _____

3. Is Noble county north or south of Shelby county? _____

4. What seven counties border on Jackson county?

   _____ _____

   _____ _____

   _____ _____

   _____

5. What three counties start with an O?

   _____ _____

   _____

6. In what county can Indianapolis be found?

   _____

7. How many counties border on Ohio?

   _____

8. Steuben county borders on which two states?

   _____ and _____

9. In what corner of the state can Switzerland county be found? _____

Discussion Topic

Most Indiana counties are square or rectangular. Why do you think some counties, like Perry, Knox, and Washington have irregular boundaries?

Although Oregon is nearly three times larger than Indiana, Oregon has only 36 counties compared with 92 for Indiana.

Where Is Switzerland When It's Not in Indiana?

A map showing the continent of Europe with countries and major cities labeled is another type of **political map**. Europe includes 43 separate countries, the Faeroe Islands, part of Russia and part of Turkey. All of Europe is in the Northern Hemisphere.

Use the map of Europe on the following page to answer these questions:

1. What four countries border on Switzerland? _____ _____
    _____ _____

2. What sea forms the eastern border of Italy? _____

3. What is the capital of Poland? _____

4. Helsinki is the capital of which country? _____

5. Is Hungary east or west of Romania? _____

6. People who live in Denmark are called Danes. What is the capital of Denmark? _____

7. The Netherlands is sometimes called Holland. What country forms the eastern border of the Netherlands? _____

8. Which country is larger, France or Belgium? _____

9. Which country is further east, Spain or Portugal? _____

Use markers, crayons or colored pencils to show these countries on the map of Europe on the next page.

10. Find Estonia, Latvia and Lithuania. Color them green.

11. Parts of Finland, Sweden, Norway and Russia are north of the Arctic Circle. Color these countries purple.

12. Italy, France and Spain are on the Mediterranean Sea. Color these countries and the islands in the Mediterranean blue.

13. The Ukraine, Belarus, Georgia, Azerbaijan and Russia were once part of the U.S.S.R. Color these countries red.

14. The United Kingdom is made up of England, Scotland, Wales and Northern Ireland. Color these countries brown.

Discussion Topic

When using a political map, why is it important to look at a current map rather than one that is five or ten years old?

Europe covers over 4 million square miles—about 7% of the world's land and contains almost 11% of the world's population.

The Continent of Europe Map

Asia, the Largest Continent

Asia is the largest of the seven continents and includes about 33% of the Earth's total land mass and 60% of the world's total population. It includes 40 countries and parts of Russia, Turkey and Egypt.

Use the map of Asia on the next page to complete this activity.

The highest point in Asia is Mount Everest: 29,028 feet above sea level. The lowest point is along the shore of the Dead Sea, 1,296 feet below sea level. Circle these two places on the map.

The borders of Asia are not as distinct as those of North America or Africa. Draw a line in black pencil or crayon to mark the traditional boundaries.

The boundary between Europe and Asia is drawn on an imaginary line passing down the spine of the Ural Mountains and through the Caspian Sea, Caucasus Mountains and Black Sea.

Asia is divided from Africa along the Suez Canal.

The boundary between Australia and Asia is drawn between the island of New Guinea and Australia.

The countries of Asia are usually grouped into five main geological subdivisions. Use crayons, markers or colored pencils to show the five subdivisions on the map.

1. **Southwest Asia.** Color this section blue. Southwest Asia includes Afghanistan, Armenia, Azerbaijan, Bahrain, Cyprus, Georgia, Iran, Iraq, Israel, Jordan, Kuwait, Lebanon, Oman, Qatar, Saudi Arabia, Syria, United Arab Emirates, Yemen, plus the parts of Turkey and Egypt east of the Suez Canal.

2. **South Asia.** Color this section green. South Asia includes Bangladesh, Bhutan, India, Maldives, Nepal, Pakistan and Sri Lanka.

3. **East Asia.** Color this section red. East Asia includes Japan, North Korea, South Korea, Taiwan and most of China. See the listing for Central and North Asia to learn which parts of China are not considered part of East Asia.

4. **Southeast Asia.** Color this section yellow. Southeast Asia includes Brunei, Burma (Myanmar), Cambodia, Indonesia, Laos, Malaysia, the Philippines, Singapore, Thailand and Vietnam.

5. **Central and North Asia.** Color this section orange. Central and North Asia includes Kazakhstan, Kyrgyzstan, Mongolia, Tajikistan, Turkmenistan and Uzbekistan, plus Asian Russian (the area known as Siberia) and three parts of China; Inner Mongolia, Tibet and Xinjiang-Uygur.

The Continent of Asia Map

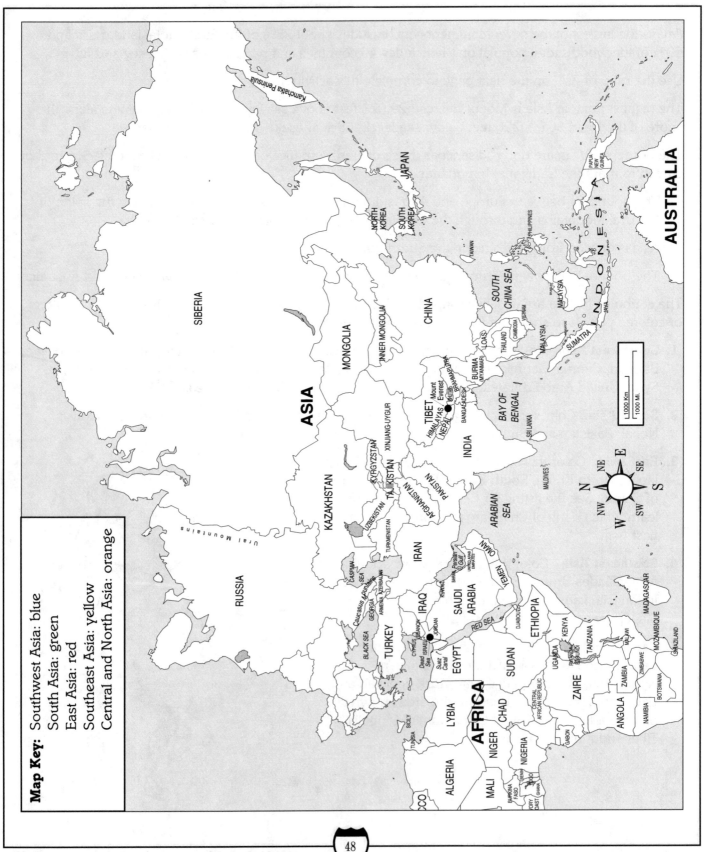

Map Key: Southwest Asia: blue
South Asia: green
East Asia: red
Southeast Asia: yellow
Central and North Asia: orange

Turn Right on Yum Yum Street

City maps contain more details than maps of larger areas. Street names, important buildings, city parks, bus routes and streams can be shown on a city map. You can often find a city map in the telephone book or get one from the local bus company.

Look at a map of your city. What types of information are shown on the map?

_____

_____

City maps can be useful to firefighters, taxi drivers and tourists. Name other people who would find a city map useful.

_____

_____

Complete this city map.

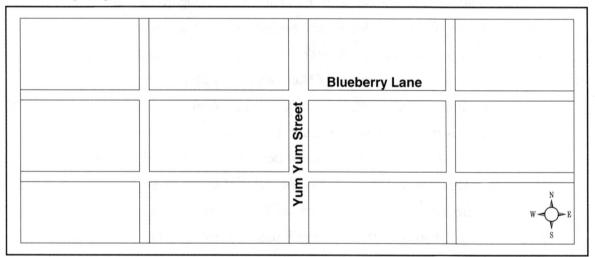

1. Popcorn Avenue crosses Blueberry Lane east of Yum Yum Street. Label Popcorn Avenue on the map.

2. Peppermint Place is west of Yum Yum Street and runs parallel to it. Label Peppermint Place.

3. Josh lives at the northeast corner of Popcorn Avenue and Banana Boulevard. Make a large *J* to show where Josh lives.

4. Rosa lives on the southwest corner of Blueberry Lane and Yum Yum Street. Make a large *R* to show where Rosa lives.

5. Josh leaves home and walks two blocks west and one block north. Make a large *X* to show where Josh is now.

6. A new park is planned on the southeast corner of Blueberry Lane and Popcorn Avenue. Make a large *P* to show where the park will be located.

Smalltown, U.S.A.

Use the map of Smalltown, U.S.A. on the next page to complete the activities below.

1. Color Mill Pond blue.
2. Color Red Wolf Creek red.
3. Draw a book on the south corner of Roosevelt and First to show the location of the library.
4. Draw the a symbol for the Smalltown swimming pool on Linden between Jefferson and Adams.
5. Draw a fish on the southeast part of Mill Pond to show the best fishing spot.

Write the number of the location of these places on the blanks.

A. _____   The Post Office is south of Jefferson Boulevard on Maple Lane.

B. _____   The Stamp Museum is on Iowa Avenue, east of Linden Lane.

C. _____   Smalltown News is on the corner of Wisconsin Avenue and Third Street.

D. _____   Washington Playground is between First and Second Streets on Washington Boulevard.

E. _____   The Sock Factory is on the corner of Elm Lane and Michigan Avenue.

F. _____   The Safe Money Bank is on Wisconsin Avenue, east of Hickory Lane.

G. _____   Kennedy Playground is on the corner of Kennedy Boulevard and Hickory Lane.

H. _____   Main Street Plaza is on the corner of Main Street and Elm Lane.

I. _____   The Hockey Rink is east of Mill Pond on Oklahoma Avenue.

J. _____   Virtual Reality Arcade is on Iowa Avenue, east of Second Street.

K. _____   Three-D Movie House is on the corner of Delaware Avenue and Division Street.

L. _____   Hamburger Haven is on Delaware Avenue, west of Maple Lane.

M. _____   Red Wolf School is east of Hickory Lane on Washington Boulevard.

N. _____   Kennedy Junior High is on the corner of Kennedy Boulevard and Maple Lane.

O. _____   Smalltown Senior High is north of the hockey rink on Delaware Avenue.

Answer these questions:

P. _____   Is Oklahoma Avenue north or south of Main Street?

Q. _____   Is Maple Lane east or west of Division Street?

R. _____   Does Adams Boulevard run parallel to Illinois Avenue?

S. _____   Does Polk Boulevard run parallel to Third Street?

I'm heading for Ye Olde Ice Cream Shoppe on Roosevelt and Third. Want to join me?

In pencil, trace the shortest route from Hamburger Haven to the Washington Playground.

Smalltown, U.S.A. Map

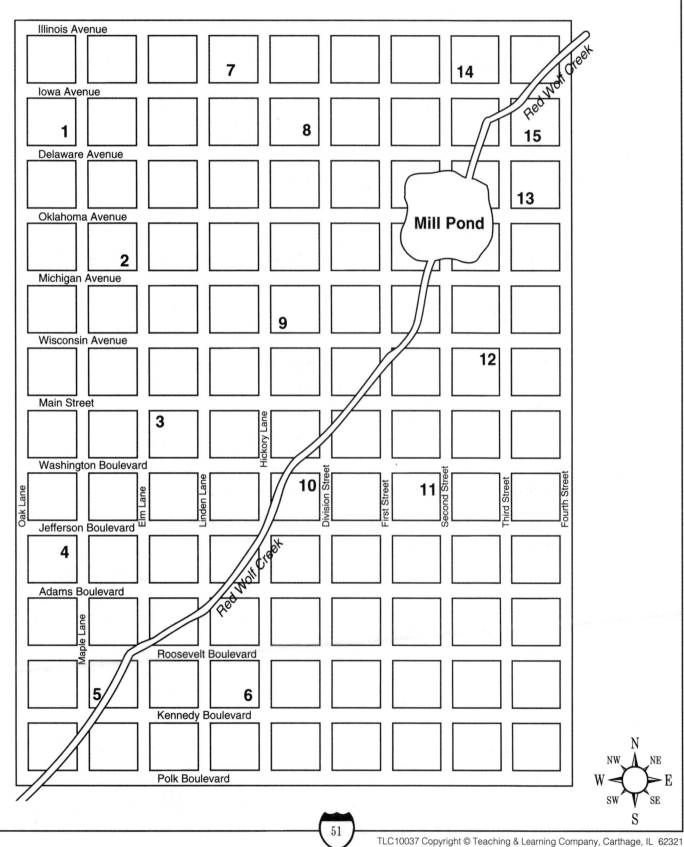

Meet Me in St. Louis, Louis

Some maps include **inset maps** which show enlargements of specific cities or areas. Inset maps usually have a separate scale, different than the one used for the main map.

Look at the inset map on the Missouri state map below.

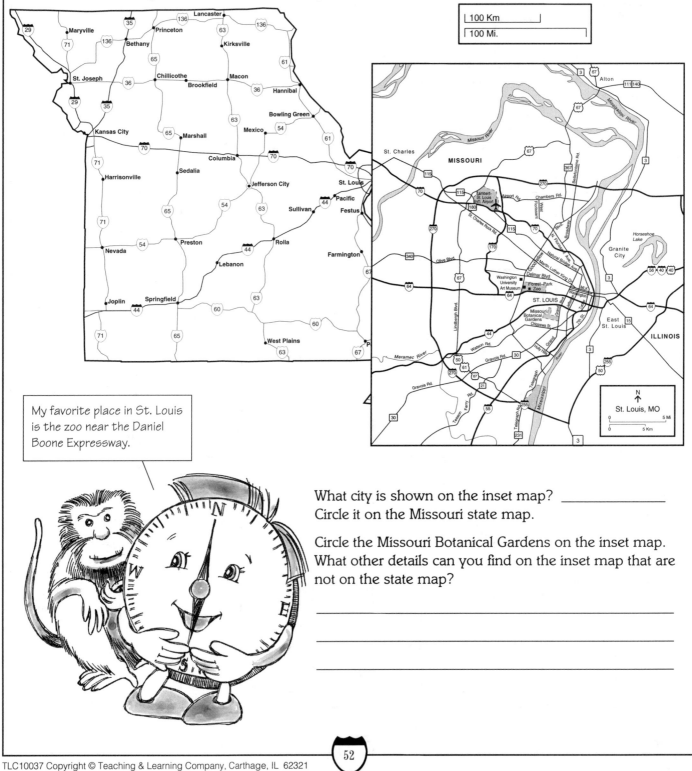

My favorite place in St. Louis is the zoo near the Daniel Boone Expressway.

What city is shown on the inset map? _____
Circle it on the Missouri state map.

Circle the Missouri Botanical Gardens on the inset map. What other details can you find on the inset map that are not on the state map?

_____

_____

52

Using What You've Learned

You've learned quite a bit about globes and maps. Let's review some of the terms and concepts.

Discussion Topics

1. What is a map? What is a globe?

2. Which is more accurate, a flat map or a globe? Why?

3. What is an atlas used for? What can you find in an atlas besides maps?

4. How do grids help you locate places on a map?

5. Do lines of latitude run parallel or perpendicular to the equator?

6. Why aren't lines of meridians equal distances apart at all places on a globe?

7. Why is the Earth divided into time zones?

8. What does a map scale show?

9. Why is a map scale different on most maps?

10. What does a map key show?

11. What kinds of information would you find on a political map?

12. How can you tell the size of cities on a map?

I think my map will show the way to the best pizza place in town.

Your Own Map

Using what you've learned about maps, drawing one should be easy. On another sheet of paper, draw a map showing how to get from your home to someplace in your community. Use a ruler to draw straight lines.

- Remember, a map is a view of an area from above.

- Label streets, buildings and other landmarks, like playgrounds, parks, creeks or rivers.

- Include a map key and a scale.

- Don't forget to show which direction is north.

- You can use color if you'd like.

- Be as detailed as you can.

Physical Maps

Physical maps may show land and water, mountains, hills, valleys, forests and deserts. You'll find large natural features like the Grand Canyon, Sahara Desert and the Great Salt Lake. Some physical maps show people-made features like roads and bridges. Some types of physical maps show how land is used.

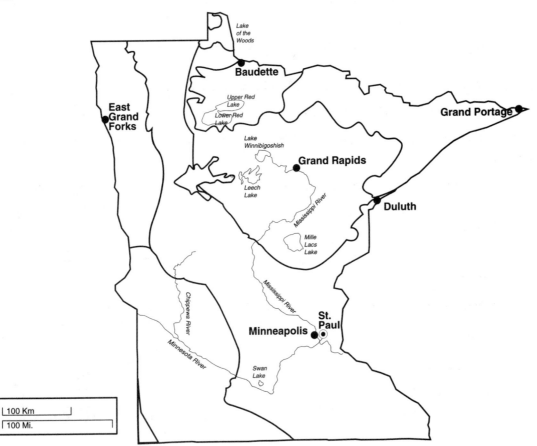

Use the map key and the Minnesota state map to complete this activity. Use crayons, markers or colored pencils to color the map.

Forest areas	dark green
General farming and wheat	light green
Dairy and livestock	orange
Dairy, hay, potatoes	dark yellow
Cattle, feed and hogs	light yellow
Livestock and grain	red
Swamplands	pink
Bodies of water, rivers	blue

54

The Land Down Under

Australia is the smallest of the seven continents and the only continent that consists of a single nation. Australia lies completely south of the equator, giving it the nickname, the Land Down Under. The continent's isolation accounts for its unique vegetation and animals.

Use crayons, markers or colored pencils with the physical map of Australia on the following page to complete this activity.

About 9% of Australia is covered with tropical rain forests, primarily along the northeastern coast. Color these areas purple.

Subtropical evergreen forests cover parts of the southeastern coast and parts of Tasmania. Over 600 species of eucalyptus trees and 800 species of acacia trees grow here. Color these areas dark green.

Chapparal or Mediterranean scrub is found in several places in the southern part of Australia. Color these areas light green.

Tropical grasslands and savannahs cover areas along the northern and northeastern coast. Color these areas dark yellow.

Much of the interior of Australia is semidesert. Color this portion light yellow.

Areas of desert known as the Outback receive less than two inches of rain a year. Very few people live in this area. Color the desert areas brown.

Use a world atlas to locate these Australian cities. Write the names of the cities in the correct places on the map.

Adelaid	Canberra	Darwin	Melbourne	Sydney
Brisbane	Cairns	Geelong	Newcastle	Townsville
Bunbury	Cooktown	Hobart	Perth	Wagga Wagga

Discussion Topic

As you look at a map of Australia, you will notice that most cities are located within a few hundred miles of the coast. Few cities, and no large ones, are located in the interior of Australia. Why do you think few people live in the central part of the continent?

The Continent of Australia Map

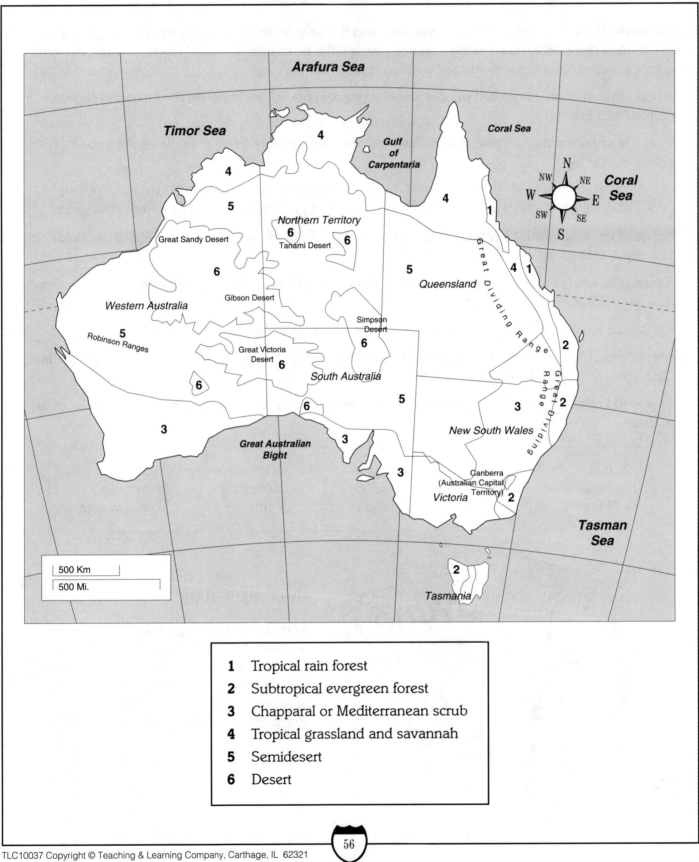

1 Tropical rain forest

2 Subtropical evergreen forest

3 Chapparal or Mediterranean scrub

4 Tropical grassland and savannah

5 Semidesert

6 Desert

How High Is Up?

Maps tell you the distance and direction from one place to another. Some physical maps can also tell you the **elevation** (how high the land is) at certain points.

Elevation maps show the height of the land below or above sea level. **Sea level** is designated as zero feet. Numbers giving the height at a particular place are called **spot heights**.

1. Look at the map of Canada on the next page. Use an atlas to find the names of the 10 provinces and two territories of Canada. Label them on the map.

2. Find the places listed below on the Canada map. Look for the numbers in italics near the names of the cities. These numbers are spot heights—the elevation at certain places.

3. Write the elevation for each city on the blank. The name of the province or territory is given to help you find the cities.

City	Province or Territory	Elevation	City	Province or Territory	Elevation
1. Belleville	Ontario	_____	16. Sydney	Nova Scotia	_____
2. Brandon	Manitoba	_____	17. Vancouver	British Columbia	_____
3. Calgary	Alberta	_____	18. Whitehorse	Yukon	_____
4. Charlottetown	Prince Edward Island	_____	19. Winnipeg	Manitoba	_____
5. Dawson	Yukon	_____	20. Yellowknife	Northwest Territory	_____
6. Edmonton	Alberta	_____			
7. Kitchener	Ontario	_____			
8. Montreal	Quebec	_____			
9. Moose Jaw	Saskatchewan	_____			
10. Niagara Falls	Ontario	_____			
11. Ottawa	Ontario	_____			
12. Prince Rupert	British Columbia	_____			
13. St. John	New Brunswick	_____			
14. St. John's	Newfoundland	_____			
15. Saskatoon	Saskatchewan	_____			

Mount Everest is the highest mountain on Earth—29,028 feet above sea level at its peak.

Canada Map

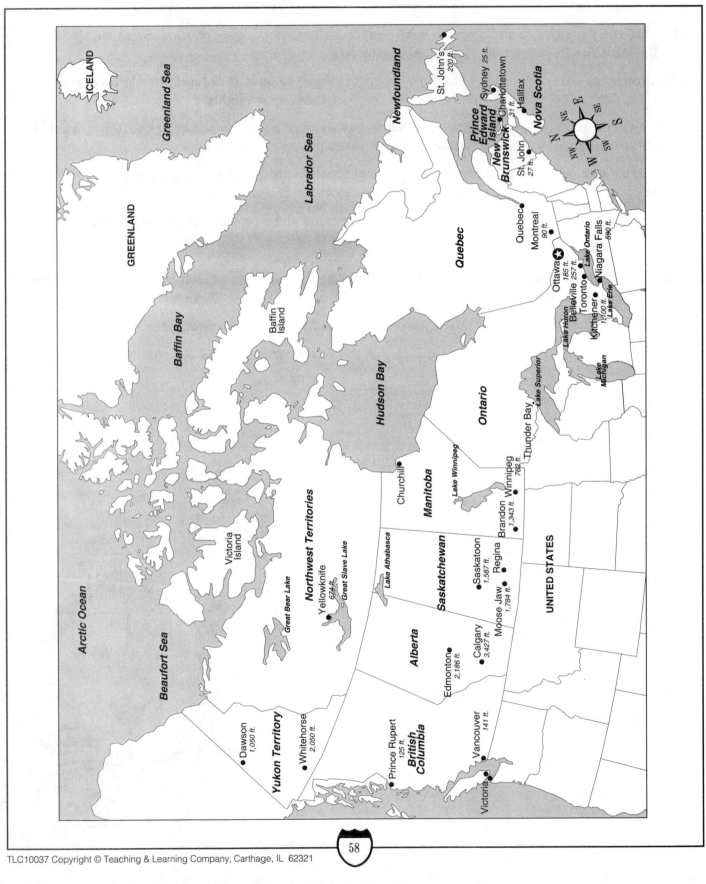

The Highs and Lows

Showing **elevation** (height of the land) of mountains and valleys can be done several ways on physical maps. One way to display the height of a mountain would be to show a cross section like this:

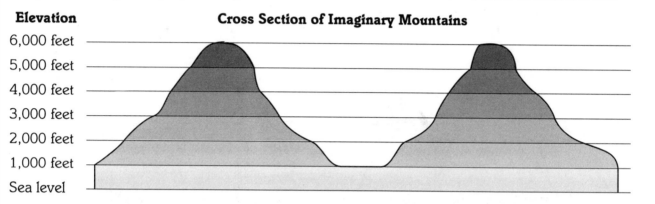

Cross Section of Imaginary Mountains

Elevation

6,000 feet
5,000 feet
4,000 feet
3,000 feet
2,000 feet
1,000 feet
Sea level

Another way to display this information is by using contour lines. Contour lines show the height of the land as viewed from above. Using contour lines, Imaginary Mountain would look like this:

Contour Map of Imaginary Mountains

Remember: When contour lines appear far apart, the land is flat. When contour lines appear close together, the land is steep. Round contour lines show the top of a hill or mountain.

Discussion Topics

1. How are the cross-section map and the contour map alike? How are they different?

2. Which gives a better picture, the cross-section map or the contour map? Why?

How Low Does It Go?

Imagine removing all the water from every lake, river, ocean and sea in the world. Would the bottom of the oceans be flat and smooth? No. The surface under water looks much like the land—filled with flat plains, mountains and valleys. The deepest valley, called the Mariana Trench is 36,198 feet below sea level. Islands like Hawaii are really mountains that are so high they show above the surface of the ocean.

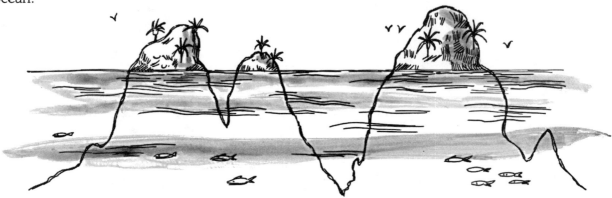

Undersea maps are called charts. They show the depths of the water much the same way as maps show the heights of land. Depths can be shown with spot heights, cross-section views or contour lines. Various shades of blue are often used on sea charts. The darker the color, the deeper the water.

Discussion Topics

1. Why would sailors need to know about the depth of water in different places?

2. How do you think the depth of the water affects undersea plants and animals?

3. Why do you think people who fish would want to know the depth of the water?

Why do you think measuring the depths of oceans would be more difficult than measuring the height of land?

_____

_____

The Mariana Trench is about seven times deeper than the Grand Canyon.

How It's Done
The depth of the oceans have been mapped using echo-sounders. These instruments send down sound waves and measure the amount of time it takes for the echo to bounce back. Because the speed of sound in known, the depth of the ocean at various points can be calculated.

Mexico

Mexico is divided into 31 states and one federal district, Mexico City. Mexico City is the capital and largest city.

Topographical maps show the elevation of land by using various colors or shading. Look in a world atlas or encyclopedia for a topographical map of Mexico. Notice how the different colors indicate different land heights.

Use the map key of the topographical map to find the elevation of the cities shown on the map below. Write the approximate height, in feet, in the blank by each city.

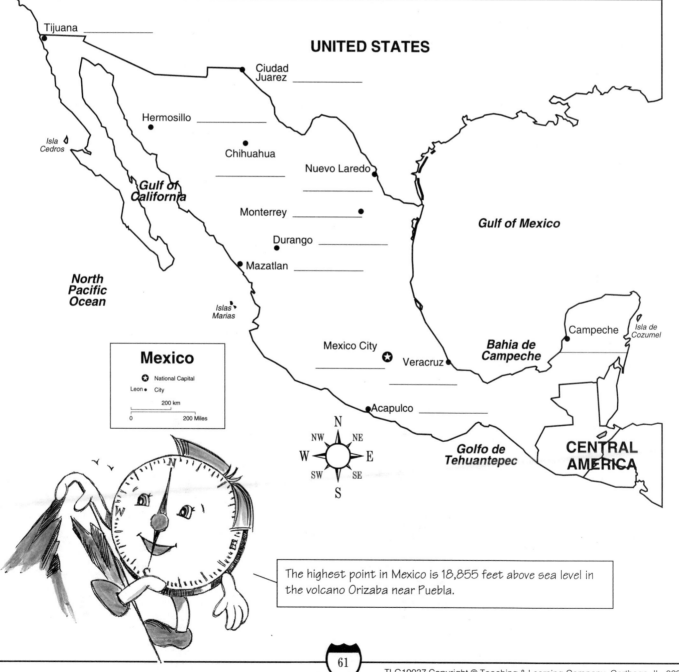

The highest point in Mexico is 18,855 feet above sea level in the volcano Orizaba near Puebla.

Specialty Maps

Specialty maps provide detailed information about

   . . . weather

   . . . climate and rainfall

   . . . crops, minerals or animals

   . . . population density (number of people in an area)

   . . . occupations

   . . . natural resources

   . . . national or state parks

   . . . ice cream consumption in a given area

What are three other types of detailed information you could find on a specialty map?

_____

_____

_____

Look at the specialty maps shown below. What types of information do these maps provide?

_____

_____

_____

_____

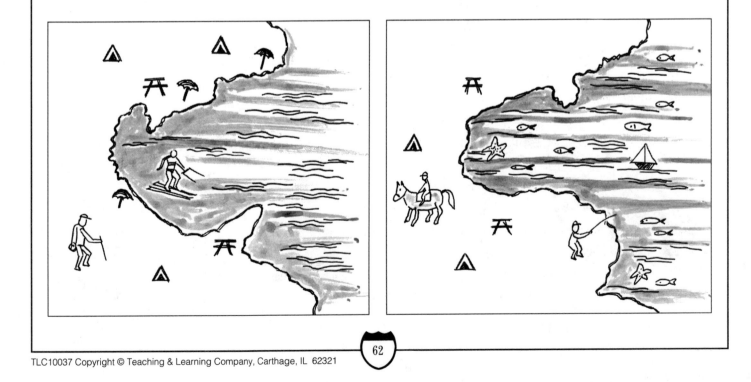

A Look at South America

One type of **specialty map** shows population density—the average number of people per square mile in a given area.

Use crayons, markers or colored pencils to show the population density of these South American countries on the map on the next page. Color each country the correct color using the information in the map key.

Map Key
People per square mile:

Less than 10:	yellow	51-60:	pink
10-20:	light green	61-70:	orange
21-30:	light blue	71-80:	red
31-40:	dark green	81-90:	grey
41-50:	dark blue	91-100:	purple

Country	People per square mile	Country	People per square mile	Country	People per square mile
Argentina	31.0	Ecuador	91.3	Peru	45.2
Bolivia	18.4	Falkland Islands	.4	Suriname	6.9
Brazil	45.9	French Guiana	3.0	Uruguay	46.0
Chile	46.5	Guyana	9.7	Venezuela	53.6
Colombia	77.9	Paraguay	28.8		

South America is one of the seven **continents**—a large land mass surrounded by water. Use the map of South America on the next page to answer these questions:

1. What is the largest country in South America? _____

2. What ocean borders South America on the west? _____

3. Montevideo is the capital of which country? _____

4. Is most of South America north or south of the equator? _____

5. Is Venezuela north or south of the equator? _____

6. Which direction would you go to get from Argentina to Bolivia?

   _____

7. What ocean borders South America on the east? _____

8. Of Guyana, Suriname and French Guiana, which country is the smallest? _____

9. What is the capital of Peru? _____

10. The equator crosses which three countries in South America?

    _____ _____ _____

The Continent of South America Map

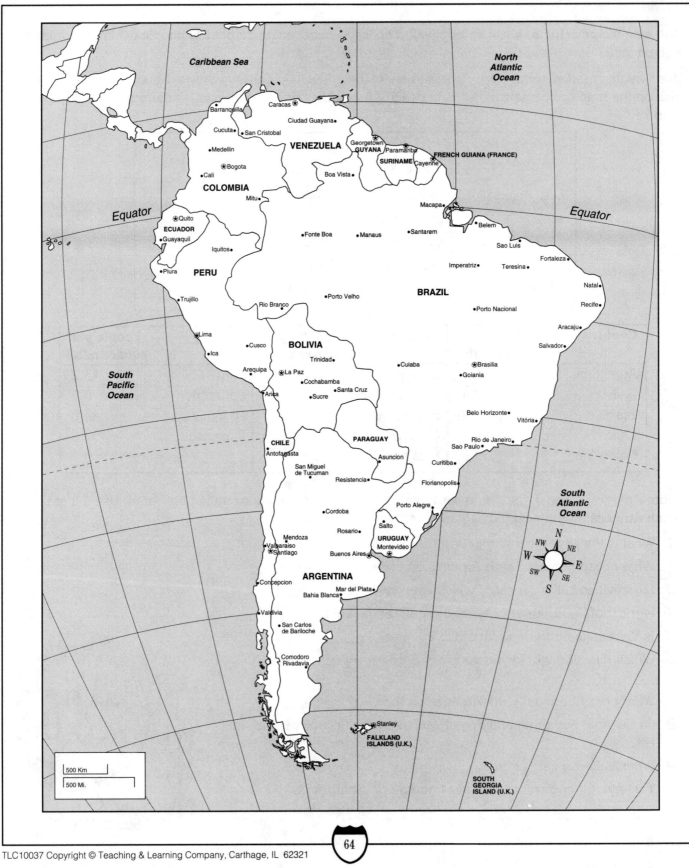

Lots of People

Some specialty maps show **population density**; the number of people per square mile in a given area. Other maps show **population changes** over a specific time period.

The population of eight California cities, is shown for 1980 and 1990 followed by the percent of increase during that 10-year period.

City	1980	1990	Percent Increase
1. Fresno	217,500	354,000	62.9%
2. Sacramento	276,000	369,500	34%
3. San Diego	875,500	1,110,500	26.8%
4. San Jose	629,500	782,000	24.3%
5. Long Beach	361,500	429,500	18.8%
6. Los Angeles	2,968,500	3,485,500	17.4%
7. Oakland	339,000	372,000	9.7%
8. San Francisco	679,000	724,000	6.6%

Near the name of the appropriate city, show the percent the population has increased using the symbols in the map key.

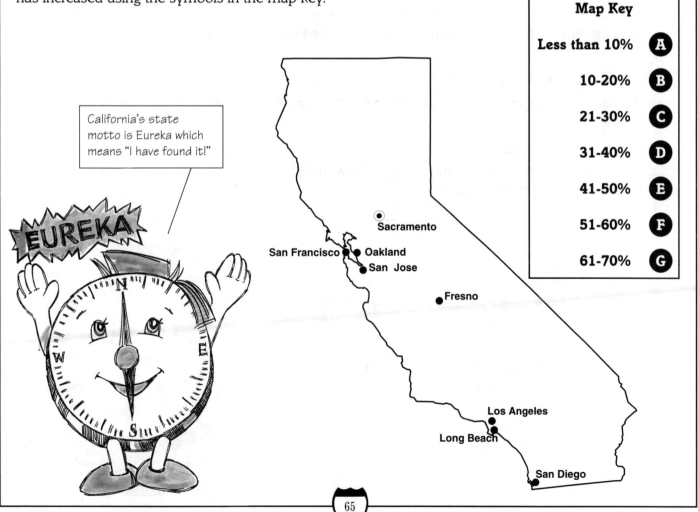

California's state motto is Eureka which means "I have found it!"

EUREKA

Map Key

Less than 10%   **A**

10-20%   **B**

21-30%   **C**

31-40%   **D**

41-50%   **E**

51-60%   **F**

61-70%   **G**

Comparison Maps

Two or more specialty maps can be used together to compare the same feature for different places. For example, a pair of maps could show the average temperature in July in France and Brazil.

Maps could also compare the same feature for the same place at different times. For example: the average temperature in Nepal in July and the average temperature in Nepal in January. Another example would be the amount of forest land in Virginia in 1700, 1800 and 1900.

Read the information below. Tell whether you'd use a single map or comparison map to portray the information listed. Explain your answer.

Would you use one map or comparison maps to show the top 10 dairy products produced in Wisconsin in 1995? Why?

_____

Would you use one map or comparison maps to show the sales of Fords in each state in 1910? Why?

_____

Would you use one map or comparison maps to show the amount of January snowfall in India in 1900 and 1950? Why?

_____

Would you use one map or comparison maps to show the location of volcanoes around the world. Why?

_____

Would you use one map or comparison maps to show routes taken by Columbus on his three voyages to the New World? Why?

_____

Would you use one map or comparison maps to show the location of active volcanoes in 1000 BC, 1000 AD, 1500 AD and today? Why?

_____

Discussion Topics

1. Why do you think it would sometimes be useful to show information on several maps rather than putting everything on one map?

2. Give some examples of information that could be shown on comparison maps.

My How We've Grown

To show population changes in an area over a given period of time, you could make a graph. The chart below shows the population of five states in 1860, 1900, 1960 and 1990.

State	1860	1900	1960	1990
Wisconsin	775,800	2,069,000	3,951,800	4,906,700
Michigan	749,000	2,421,000	7,823,200	9,328,800
Minnesota	172,000	1,751,400	3,413,900	4,387,000
Illinois	1,712,000	4,821,600	10,081,200	11,466,700
Iowa	674,900	2,231,900	2,757,500	2,787,400

Transfer the information to the graph below. Wisconsin has been done as an example.

Population Changes, 1860-1990

	Wisconsin	Michigan	Minnesota	Illinois	Iowa
10,000,000					
9,500,000					
9,000,000					
8,500,000					
8,000,000					
7,500,000					
7,000,000					
6,500,000					
6,000,000					
5,500,000					
5,000,000					
4,500,000					
4,000,000					
3,500,000					
3,000,000					
2,500,000					
2,000,000					
1,500,000					
1,000,000					
500,000					

1860 1900 1960 1990 1860 1900 1960 1990 1860 1900 1960 1990 1860 1900 1960 1990 1860 1900 1960 1990

This information could also be displayed on comparison maps.

Use crayons, markers or colored pencils to color in the states on all four maps on the next page. Use the correct color based on the state population for the year.

Red	Over 10,000,000	Green	500,000-1,000,000
Pink	5,000,000-10,000,000	Yellow	100,000-500,000
Blue	1,000,000-5,000,000		

My How We've Grown

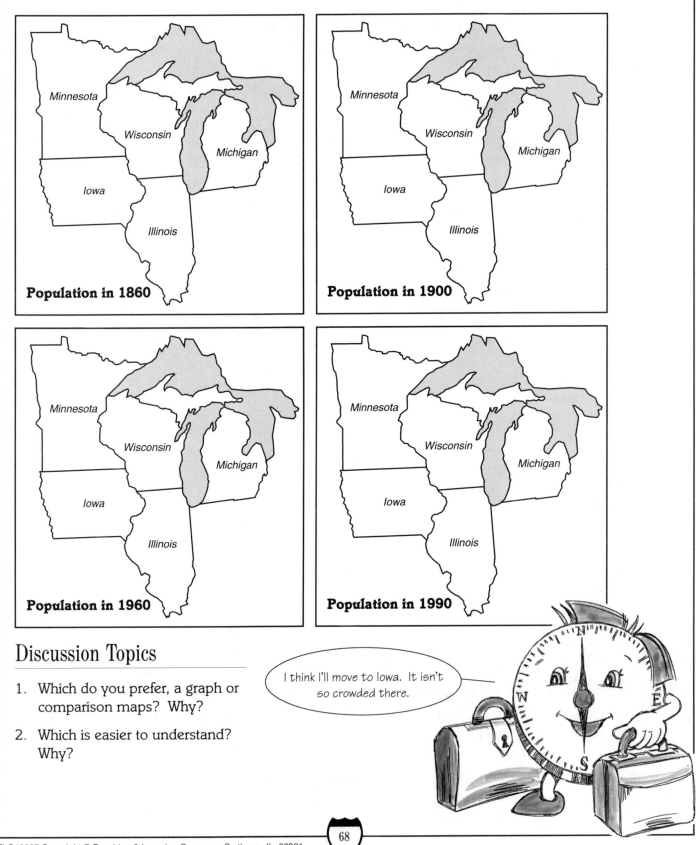

Population in 1860

Population in 1900

Population in 1960

Population in 1990

Discussion Topics

1. Which do you prefer, a graph or comparison maps? Why?

2. Which is easier to understand? Why?

> I think I'll move to Iowa. It isn't so crowded there.

Product Maps

Product maps show agricultural and other natural resources produced in an area.

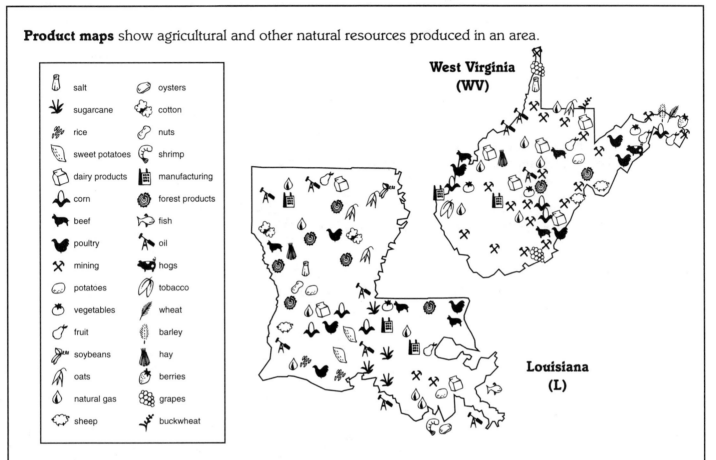

salt		oysters	
sugarcane		cotton	
rice		nuts	
sweet potatoes		shrimp	
dairy products		manufacturing	
corn		forest products	
beef		fish	
poultry		oil	
mining		hogs	
potatoes		tobacco	
vegetables		wheat	
fruit		barley	
soybeans		hay	
oats		berries	
natural gas		grapes	
sheep		buckwheat	

West Virginia (WV)

Louisiana (L)

Look at the maps showing major products in Louisiana and West Virginia. Answer the questions below. Write *L* for Louisiana or *WV* for West Virginia in the blanks.

1. _____ Which state has more mining?

2. _____ Which state produces more cotton?

3 _____ In which state are hogs an important product?

4. _____ Which state is a tobacco producer?

5. _____ In which state is fishing more important?

6. _____ In which state are wheat and barley more important?

7. _____ Which state is a rice producer?

8. _____ Which state produces sugarcane and sweet potatoes?

9. _____ Which state produces berries and grapes?

10. _____ Which state has more shrimp boats?

11. _____ In which state would you be more likely to find oysters?

12. _____ Soybeans are a major crop in which state?

Where Does All the Corn Grow?

Maps can show which states are the leading producers of certain crops. This type of specialty map is called a **product map**.

 The five top corn-producing states in 1991 were Iowa, Illinois, Nebraska, Minnesota and Indiana. Draw a small ear of corn in these states on the map.

 The five top wheat-producing states in 1991 were Kansas, North Dakota, Oklahoma, Washington and Montana. Draw a stalk of wheat in these states.

The five top cotton-producing states in 1991 were Texas, California, Mississippi, Louisiana and Arkansas. Draw a boll of cotton in these states.

The top five potato-producing states in 1991 were Idaho, Washington, Colorado, Wisconsin and Oregon. Draw a potato in these states.

Corn: An Important Crop Around the World

Corn is an important crop all over the world. One way to present information about how much corn is produced is to use a graph like the one below. It shows the top corn-producing countries and how many metric tons of corn they produce every year.

Top Corn-Producing Countries		(Metric Tons)					
		50,000,000	75,000,000	100,000,000	150,000,000	175,000,000	200,000,000
United States	189,867,000						
China	93,345,500						
Brazil	22,604,000						
Mexico	13,527,000						
France	12,787,000						
Romania	10,493,000						
South Africa	8,200,000						
India	8,200,000						
Argentina	7,768,000						
Hungary	7,509,000						
Canada	7,319,000						
Indonesia	6,409,000						
Italy	6,208,000						
Egypt	5,270,000						
Philippines	4,655,000						

Another visual way to show this information would be by putting it on a world map.

What would be some advantages of using a map rather than a graph like the one above?

_____

What would be some disadvantages of using a map rather than a graph like the one above?

_____

Explain how you would transfer the information about the top corn-producing countries to a map. How would you show how much corn each country produced?

_____

_____

Corn bread, popcorn, tortillas, corn on the cob, I get hungry thinking about all the good things made from corn.

Weather Maps

Weather maps show the forecast for a given time period for a specific area. The map may show the expected high and low temperatures, whether it will be sunny or cloudy, and whether it will rain, snow, sleet or hail.

Study a daily weather map from a newspaper. What symbols are used and what do they mean?

_____

How are high and low temperatures shown? _____

_____

What else is shown on the weather map? _____

_____

Make your own weather map using the information below. Show expected high temperatures in red and lows in blue. Fill in the map key with the symbols you will use for rain, snow, cloudy and sunny.

Washington: Rain expected in the western third of the state. High-70°F, low-52°F. The rest of Washington will be cloudy. High-65°F, low-45°F.

Oregon: Sunny skies will cover the state. High-72°F, low-60°F along the coast. High-68°F, low-55°F inland.

California: Sunny skies over the northern half of the state. High-80°F, low-75°F. Snow expected in the higher elevations near Lake Tahoe. High-42°F, low-37°F. Rain expected over the southern part of the state. High-60°F, low-49°F.

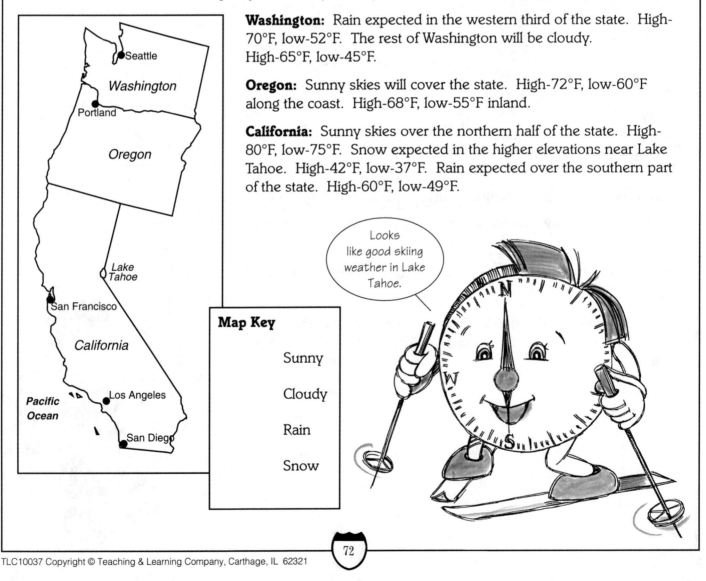

Weather and Climate

Weather changes from day to day. It can be hot and dry one day and cold and rainy the next.

The weather pattern over time for an area is called its **climate**. Scientists study weather records of temperature, precipitation, wind speeds and direction. They look at the number of sunny days and cloudy ones to form an overall picture of climate for an area.

Discussion Topic

If you know the average temperature for the year in a given place is 65°F, how much do you know about the climate? Does that mean the temperature stays between 60° and 70° all year or that it drops to below zero in winter and to over 100° in summer?

The average temperature, like the average amount of precipitation for an area tells you very little. You need to know the expected range of temperature and precipitation at different times during the year.

	City A Temperature (F)	Precipitation	City B Temperature (F)	Precipitation
January	67°	6"	-3°	8"
March	68°	8"	21°	10"
May	69°	7"	45°	4"
July	70°	6.5"	82°	3"
September	69°	7"	58°	6"
November	68°	6"	36°	9"

Answer the questions by writing an *A* for City A or a *B* for City B in the blanks.

_____ Which city gets snow sometimes?

_____ Which city has the greatest temperature change during the year?

_____ Which city gets warmer in January?

_____ Which city gets warmer in July?

_____ Which city gets more precipitation in July?

_____ Which city would you rather live in? Why?

_____

_____

_____

_____

I'd rather live in City B. I like to ski, ice skate and build snowmen.

How Hot Does It Get?

This map shows the average temperature in July in the continental United States. Use the map to answer the questions below.

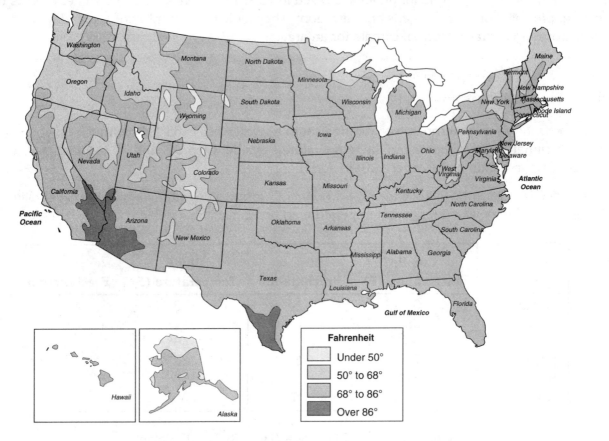

Fahrenheit
	Under 50°
	50° to 68°
	68° to 86°
	Over 86°

1. What is the average temperature in Arkansas in July? _____

2. Which four states show the highest average temperature?

   _____ _____ _____ _____

3. List three states where the average temperature in July is less than 50 in some places.

   _____ _____ _____

4. What is the average temperature in most of Maine in July?

   _____

5. Which state has a higher average temperature in July: Vermont or Oklahoma?

   _____

6. Which state has a lower average temperature in July: Louisiana or New Mexico?

   _____

How does a map like this give you an overall picture of July temperatures across the United States?

_____

On July 10, 1913, a record high temperature of 134°F was recorded in Death Valley, California.

How Cold Does It Get?

The map showing the average July temperature in the United States used shading to provide the information. Another way to provide information about climate is to show the average temperature for specific cities during a given month.

Write the average January temperature on the map near the name of the correct city.

City	Average January Temperature (F)
Albany, NY	21°
Asheville, NC	36°
Atlanta, GA	41°
Atlantic City, NJ	31°
Baltimore, MD	32°
Boston, MA	29°
Buffalo, NY	24°
Caribou, ME	9°
Charleston, SC	48°
Hartford, CT	25°
Jackonsville, FL	52°
Miami, FL	67°
Newark, NJ	31°
New York, NY	32°
Norfolk, VA	39°
Philadelphia, PA	30°
Pittsburgh, PA	26°
Portland, ME	21°
Providence, RI	28°
Raleigh, NC	39°
Richmond, VA	37°
Savannah, GA	49°
Tampa, FL	60°

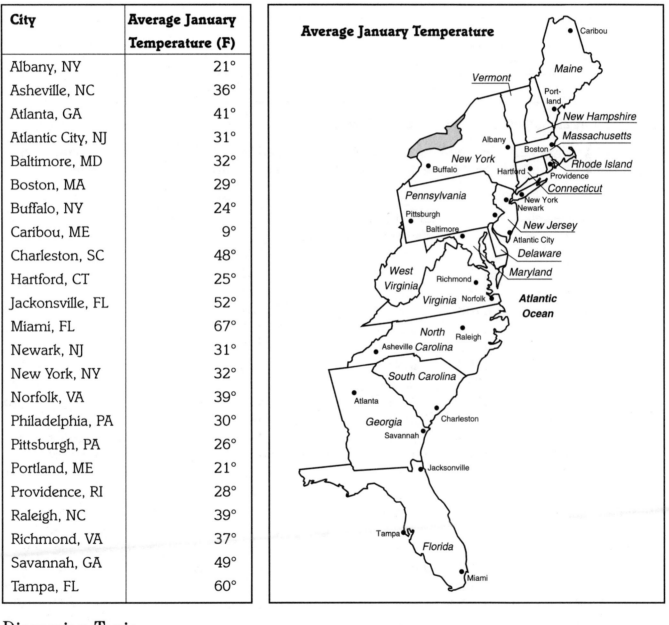

Average January Temperature

Discussion Topic

What do you notice about temperatures as you go from north to south along the coast?

TLC10037 Copyright © Teaching & Learning Company, Carthage, IL 62321

Historical Maps

A **historical map** gives a visual picture of historical events. At a glance, you can easily see an overall picture of events. Historical maps could show dates cities were founded, which countries claimed specific areas of the New World, political boundaries at different times in history or battle sites.

List four other types of information that could be found on a historical map.

_____

_____

_____

_____

Make a historical map of the United States to show when the states were admitted to the Union.

The list below shows the states and dates they joined the United States. On the U.S. map on the next page, color each state according to the directions given. Use crayons, markers or colored pencils.

Color these states yellow.
Original 13 states:

Delaware	1787
New Jersey	1787
Pennsylvania	1787
Connecticut	1788
Georgia	1788
Maryland	1788
Massachusetts	1788
New Hampshire	1788
New York	1788
South Carolina	1788
Virginia	1788
North Carolina	1789
Rhode Island	1790

Color these states red.
Admitted 1791-1800:

Vermont	1791
Kentucky	1792
Tennessee	1796

Color these states green.
Admitted 1801-1850:

Ohio	1803
Louisiana	1812
Indiana	1816
Mississippi	1817
Illinois	1818
Alabama	1819
Maine	1820
Missouri	1821
Arkansas	1836
Michigan	1837
Florida	1845
Texas	1845
Iowa	1846
Wisconsin	1848
California	1850

Color these states blue.
Admitted 1851-1900:

Minnesota	1858
Oregon	1859
Kansas	1861

West Virginia	1863
Nevada	1864
Nebraska	1867
Colorado	1876
Montana	1889
North Dakota	1889
South Dakota	1889
Washington	1889
Idaho	1890
Wyoming	1890
Utah	1896

Color these states purple.
Admitted 1901-1950:

Oklahoma	1907
Arizona	1912
New Mexico	1912

Color these states orange.
Admitted 1951-present:

Alaska	1959
Hawaii	1959

Historical Map of the United States

Color in each state according to the directions on the previous page. Then complete the map by coloring the boxes.

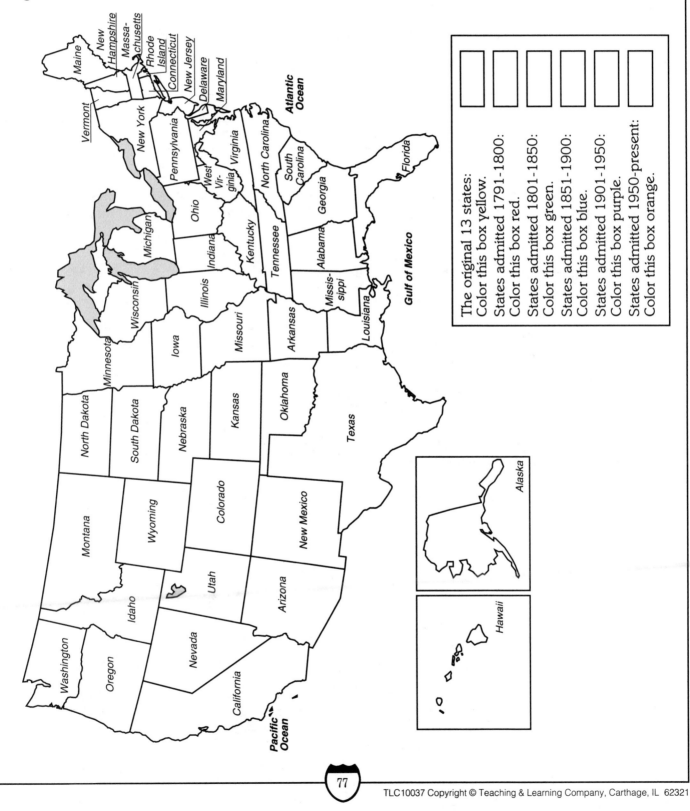

The original 13 states:
Color this box yellow.

States admitted 1791–1800:
Color this box red.

States admitted 1801–1850:
Color this box green.

States admitted 1851–1900:
Color this box blue.

States admitted 1901–1950:
Color this box purple.

States admitted 1950–present:
Color this box orange.

Would You Like to Buy the Brooklyn Bridge?

Businesses may use maps that show population density, age distribution or occupation to help them plan sales or new locations for their business. They could create their own specialty maps to show product sales in different parts of the country.

Name some other types of specialty maps businesses might use. Explain how the maps would be useful.

Type of business	Type of map	Reason it would be useful
_____	_____	_____
		_____
_____	_____	_____
		_____

The engineers at Acme Bridge Company have designed a new bridge made of recycled tires that looks like the Brooklyn Bridge. The Sales Department plans to contact the mayors of cities in Tennessee that might buy their new bridge.

You can help by finding the names of 10 cities near a river.
Write the names of the cities on the blanks below the map.

Tennessee has some towns with unusual names: Bells, Halls, Christmasville, Difficult, Friendship, Finger, Only, Wartburg, Wartrace, Gates, Mascot, Paris, Moscow and White House.

1. _____
2. _____
3. _____
4. _____
5. _____
6. _____
7. _____
8. _____
9. _____
10. _____

Sales Are Booming

As Pennsylvania state sales manager for the Hi-Lo Pogo Stick Company, you must give a presentation at the company's annual sales meeting. Since you don't like to give long speeches, you decide to prepare a map showing sales for the past year.

On the Pennsylvania map, draw one / for each 1,000 pogo sticks sold near the appropriate city. Use ⧻ to show each 5,000 pogo sticks sold. Round numbers to the nearest thousand.

City	# Sold	City	# Sold
Altoona	1,043	Imperial	3,200
Atlas	1,162	Lantz Corners	9,503
Bethlehem	7,142	Oil City	18,406
Bird in Hand	9,280	Philadelphia	14,061
Dublin	1,985	Pittsburgh	12,054
Egypt	1,369	Scranton	1,100
Erie	10,691	Towanda	900
Gettysburg	7,025	Washington	980
Harrisburg	5,784	York	4,192
Harmony	16,234	Yukon	1,987

I wonder how anyone could sell 16,234 pogo sticks in a city with only 1,054 people? Things must really be hopping in Harmony!

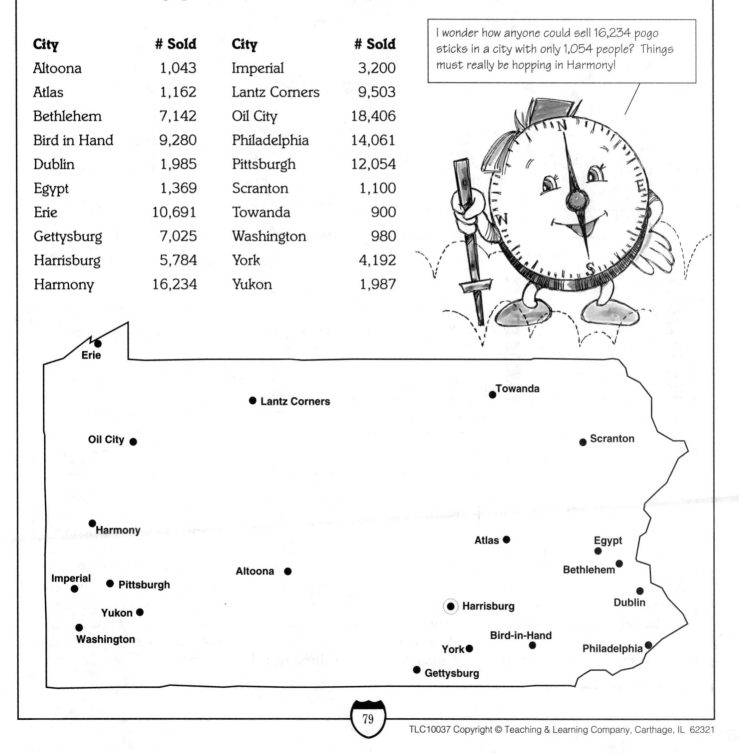

Pizza Deluxe

Papa Pio's Pizza Parlor took a survey to find out what kind of toppings people in Michigan prefer on their pizzas. Transfer the results of the survey onto the state map below. Use the symbols in the map key to show the preferred type of pizza for each city.

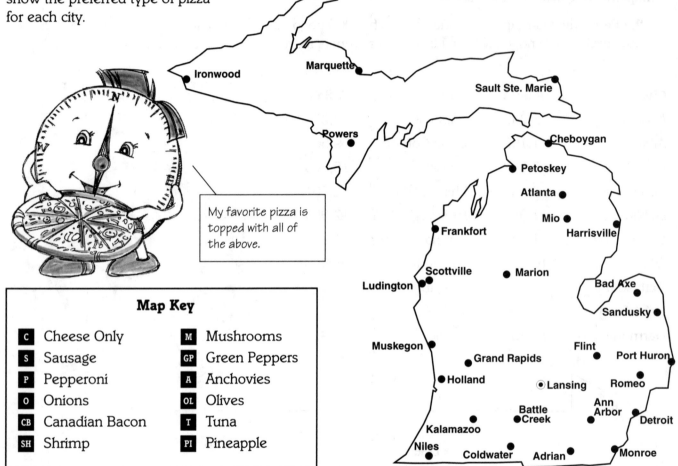

My favorite pizza is topped with all of the above.

Map Key

C	Cheese Only	**M**	Mushrooms
S	Sausage	**GP**	Green Peppers
P	Pepperoni	**A**	Anchovies
O	Onions	**OL**	Olives
CB	Canadian Bacon	**T**	Tuna
SH	Shrimp	**PI**	Pineapple

City	Topping	City	Topping	City	Topping
Kalamazoo	Onions	Monroe	Anchovies	Mio	Pineapple
Battle Creek	Cheese Only	Romeo	Sausage	Harrisville	Tuna
Ironwood	Shrimp	Powers	Onions	Adrian	Pineapple
Niles	Canadian Bacon	Grand Rapids	Tuna	Flint	Pepperoni
Ludington	Sausage	Cheboygan	Onions	Bad Axe	Canadian Bacon
Atlanta	Onions	Ann Arbor	Pepperoni	Port Huron	Anchovies
Marion	Sausage	Holland	Sausage	Marquette	Green Peppers
Coldwater	Olives	Scottville	Green Peppers	Lansing	Mushrooms
Detroit	Onions	Muskegon	Tuna	Sault Ste. Marie	Olives
Sandusky	Olives	Frankfort	Mushrooms	Petosky	Mushrooms

Know These Terms

Write the letter of the correct answer in the blanks.

1. ____ Meridian   A. A person who draws maps

2. ____ Political map   B. An instrument used to find directions

3. ____ Map   C. Shows distance on the ground compared to distance on a map

4. ____ Latitude   D. A list explaining symbols used on a map

5. ____ Coordinates   E. Small pictures that represent features on a map

6. ____ Inset map   F. A map showing an enlarged view of one area of another map

7. ____ Scale   G. The letter and number of a place on a grid

8. ____ Grid   H. A three-dimensional model of the Earth

9. ____ Map symbols   I. Imaginary lines which run at right angles to the equator

10. ____ Map key   J. Imaginary lines which parallel the equator

11. ____ Globe   K. A system of imaginary lines on a map

12. ____ Equator   L. A map showing where people live

13. ____ NW   M. A book of maps

14. ____ Historical map   N. Flat pictures of places as seen from above

15. ____ Longitude   O. Abbreviation used for *northwest*

16. ____ Population map   P. An imaginary line around the middle of the Earth

17. ____ Cartographer   Q. Another name for a line of longitude

18. ____ Atlas   R. A map of a room drawn to scale

19. ____ Floor plan   S. Gives a visual picture of historical events

20. ____ Compass   T. Shows boundaries of countries, states, counties or cities

81

Challenge Questions

This list of questions and topics includes ones students can complete as assignments or as extra credit work.

1. Learn more about one of these mapmakers: Eratosthenes of Cyrene, Hipparchus, Strabo, Ptolemy, Anaximander, Gerardus Mercator, Arthur Robinson, Juan de la Cosa, Martin Waldseemuller or Abraham Ortelius.

2. What is magnetite? What does it look like? Where can it be found? What is it used for.

3. Why does the needle on a compass always point north?

4. How does a weather vane show wind direction?

5. Wind direction can be important to people like pilots and firefighters. Why? What about people in other occupations or hobbies? Why would wind direction be important to them?

6. Draw a detailed map showing a recent trip you took.

7. How can a compass help if you are lost in the woods?

8. Compare a Mercator Projection Map to a Robinson Projection Map.

9. When it is summer in the Northern Hemisphere, it is winter in the Southern Hemisphere. Why?

10. When it is daytime in the Eastern Hemisphere, it is nighttime in the Western Hemisphere. Why?

11. Look up the latitude and longitude for these cities: Moscow, Paris, London, Buenos Aires, Mexico City, Cape Town and Miami.

12. A map is a picture of a place. How is a map like a photograph? How is it different?

13. Why is Central America considered part of the North American continent rather than part of South America?

14. How do mountains affect a country's climate?

15. Compare the average temperature and precipitation of two states for each month during a year.

16. Prepare a community map showing where students in your class live.

17. Prepare a report which includes a map. Select a topic for one of the continents. Suggestions are: climate, vegetation, mineral resources, animals, population distribution, products or land use.

18. Prepare comparison maps for two places on any topic.

Suggestions for Using Maps

Mighty Maps! includes reproducible maps of the seven continents, Mexico, Canada and the United States with specific activities. These could also be used for more intensive study or to prepare specialized maps of a specific area.

Students will need copies of the two-page world map and the two-page U.S. map for several activities.

Students could also use copies of these maps to . . .

Prepare maps showing major rivers and bodies of water.

Compare the size of various states or countries to each other.

Prepare population distribution maps.

Prepare historical maps in conjunction with a history unit.

- Trace the route of Columbus's three voyages.

- Trace Magellan's route when he circumnavigated the Earth.

- Trace the routes across the U.S. during exploration and the westward movement (Lewis and Clark explorations, Oregon Trail, Santa Fe Trail, etc.).

- Show the acquisition of territory and growth of the United States.

Prepare product maps and comparison maps.

Transfer graph information to maps.

Identify global neighbors.

Label major mountain chains, showing elevation with different colors.

Prepare a world time zone map.

Locate major islands, fault lines or volcanoes along the Ring of Fire.

Locate and identify the capitals of countries around the world.

Prepare comparison maps for specific topics related to other units being studied.

Prepare climate, rainfall and precipitation maps in conjunction with units on weather.

Locate places of interest for current events. Encourage students to write headlines on a world map near the place where an event occurred.

Study the relationship of countries to each other.

Study physical features that affect climate.

World Map

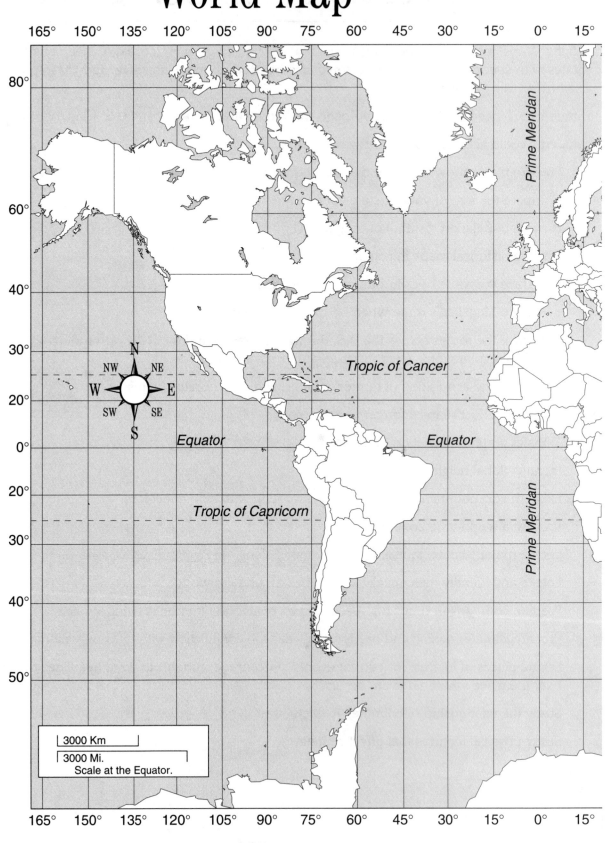

Name _____

World Map

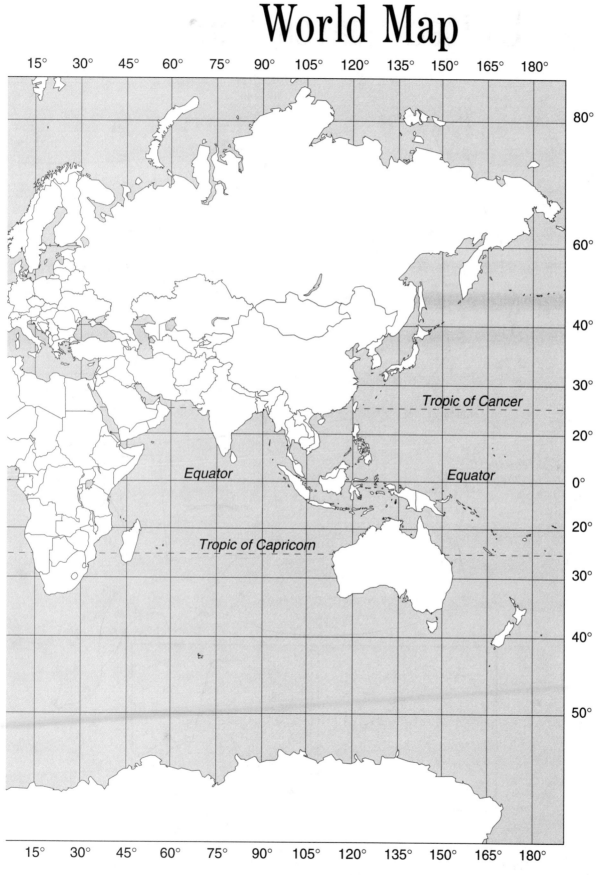

| 15° | 30° | 45° | 60° | 75° | 90° | 105° | 120° | 135° | 150° | 165° | 180° |

80°
60°
40°
30°
Tropic of Cancer
20°
Equator   Equator   0°
20°
Tropic of Capricorn
30°
40°
50°

| 15° | 30° | 45° | 60° | 75° | 90° | 105° | 120° | 135° | 150° | 165° | 180° |

85

Name _____

United States Map

Name _____

United States Map

90°   80°   70°

50°

Maine

Vermont

New Hampshire

Massachusetts

40°

esota

Wisconsin

Michigan

New York

Rhode Island

Connecticut

Iowa

Pennsylvania

New Jersey

Illinois   Indiana   Ohio

Delaware

West
Virginia

Maryland

Missouri

Virginia

Atlantic
Ocean

N
NW   NE
W   E
SW   SE
S

Kentucky

Tennessee

North Carolina

30°

Arkansas

South Carolina

Mississippi   Alabama   Georgia

Louisiana

Florida

Gulf of Mexico

Tropic of Cancer

f Cancer

20°

500 Km

500 Mi.

90°   80°   70°

North America Map

South America Map

Caribbean Sea

North Atlantic Ocean

•Barranquilla   Caracas•

Cucuta•   Ciudad Guayana•

•San Cristobal

VENEZUELA   Georgetown•
GUYANA   Paramaribo•
FRENCH GUIANA (FRANCE)

•Medellin

SURINAME   Cayenne•

•Bogota   Boa Vista•

•Cali

COLOMBIA

Macapa•

Mitu•

•Belem

• Quito   •Fonte Boa   •Manaus   •Santarem

ECUADOR

Sao Luis•

Guayaquil•   Iquitos•

Fortaleza•

•Piura   **PERU**   Imperatriz•   •Teresina

Natal•

•Trujillo   •Porto Velho   **BRAZIL**

Rio Branco•   Recife•

•Porto Nacional

Aracaju•

•Lima   •Cusco   **BOLIVIA**   Salvador•

•Ica   Trinidad•   •Cuiaba   •Brasilia

Arequipa•   •La Paz   •Goiania

South Pacific Ocean

•Arica   •Cochabamba

•Santa Cruz

•Sucre   Belo Horizonte•

Vitória•

CHILE   **PARAGUAY**   Rio de Janeiro•

Antofagasta•   •Asuncion   Sao Paulo•

San Miguel   •Curitiba

de Tucuman•   Resistencia•   Florianopolis•

•Cordoba   Porto Alegre•

•Salto

Mendoza•   Rosario•   **URUGUAY**

Valparaiso•   Buenos Aires•   •Montevideo

•Santiago

South Atlantic Ocean

•Concepcion   **ARGENTINA**   Mar del Plata•

Bahia Blanca•

•Valdivia

•San Carlos de Bariloche

•Comodoro Rivadavia

FALKLAND ISLANDS (U.K.)

500 Km

500 Mi.

SOUTH GEORGIA ISLAND (U.K.)

Answer Key

Using an Atlas, page 7

1. France; 2. Asia; 3. Africa; 4. Australia;
5. Brasília; 6. Pacific Ocean; 7. No; 8. Ceylon;
9. California; 10. Baton Rouge; 11. Oregon and
Idaho; 12. Atlantic Ocean; 13. North Dakota;
14. Mississippi; 15. Texas, New Mexico,
Arizona and California; 16. North Dakota

Land and Water, page 9

1. Asia; 2. Australia, Antarctica; 3. Europe;
4. Victoria, Wilkes, American, Enderby;
5. Victoria; 6. Enderby, Queen Maud;
7. Victoira, Ross; 8. Argentina, Chile

North, South, East, West and Points In-Between, page 12

1. north, 2. east, 3. south, 4. west
A. southeast, B. northwest, C. southwest,
D. northwest

Which Way from Omaha? page 13

1. NE, 2. SE, 3. SW, 4. SE, 5. W, 6. E, 7. NE,
8. N, 9. NW, 10. SE, 11. NE, 12. E, 13. S,
14. S, 15. SW, 16. SE, 17. SW, 18. SE, 19. NW,
20. SW

Which Way to El Dorado? page 14

1. S, 2. NW, 3. NW, 4. NE, 5. SE, 6. N, 7. NE,
8. NE, 9. NW, 10. NE, 11. NE, 12. E, 13. S,
14. SW, 15. N, 16. NW, 17. E, 18. SW, 19. S,
20. SW

X Marks the Spot, page 15

10. Xenia

Finding Your Way Around a Map, page 17

5. D2, 6. C1

Zap! You're in North Dakota, page 18

1. D3, 2. B3, 3. H2, 4. H3, 5. F3, 6. D3, 7. D2,
8. A2

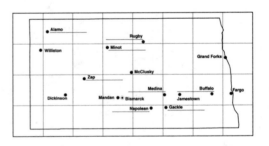

Grid Work, page 19

1. BOISE, 2. SALEM, 3. HELENA, 4. JUNEAU,
5. BOSTON, 6. AUSTIN, 7. TOPEKA,
8. PIERRE, 9. ALBANY, 10. AUGUSTA,
11. OLYMPIA, 12. PHOENIX, 13. MADISON,
14. ATLANTA, 15. LINCOLN, 16. LANSING,
17. BISMARCK, 18. HONOLULU,
19. RICHMOND, 20. COLUMBIA,
21. CHEYENNE, 22. SACRAMENTO

On a Flat Map, page 22
1. Answers will vary; 2. 40° North; 3. Iceland, Greenland; 4. 100° West; 5. 20° North

What Time Is It? page 25
1. 7 A.M., 2. noon, 3. 9 A.M., 4. noon,
5. Pacific, 6. Eastern, 7. 4 P.M., 8. 3 P.M.

How Far? pages 27-28
A. 150 miles, B. 500 miles, C. 3 inches,
D. ¾ inch. NOTE: Student answers need not be exact but should be close. 1. 400 miles,
2. 750 miles, 3. 1,150 miles, 4. 10 miles,
5. 23 miles, 6. 28 miles, 7. 600 miles,
8. 2,775 miles, 9. 1,613 miles

As the Crow Flies, page 30
1. 187, 2. 281, 3. 225, 4. 188, 5. 581, 6. 506

Colorado Vacation, page 31
Aspen—SW, 83 miles
Crested Butte National Landmark—SW, 98
Grand Junction—SW, 158
Mesa Verde National Park—SW, 203
Rocky Mountain National Park—NW, 45
Steamboat Springs—NW, 90
Vail—W, 60

Africa, page 34
1. Algiers, 2. Luanda, 3. Gaborone,
4. N'Djamena, 5. Cairo, 6. Addis Ababa,
7. Nairobi, 8. Monrovia, 9. Bamako,
10. Niamey, 11. Freetown, 12. Mogadishu,
13. Kampala, 14. Kinshasa, 15. west,
16. Atlantic, 17. south, 18. Madagascar,
19. Mediterranean, 20. Somalia, Kenya,
Uganda, Zaire, Congo, Gabon

City Size, page 36
1. Haverhill, 2. Framingham, 3. Fitchburg,
4. Holyoke, 5. New Bedford, 6. Boston,
7. Springfield, 8. Haverhill, 9. Quincy,
10. Attleboro

Let's Visit Yellowstone National Park, page 38
2. Black Sand Basin, Biscuit Basin, Midway Geyser Basin, Lower Geyser Basin; 4. Firehole River; 5. picnic area; 6. 15 miles; 7. no;
8. Canyon Village; 9. Lower Falls;
11. Yellowstone Lake; 12. Bridge Bay;
13. Natural Bridge; 14. Grant Village

Road Maps, page 40

1. (84)

2. (191)

3. ············

4. ▲

5. I-15; 6. U.S. 40, U.S. highway; 7. ～ , answers may vary; 9. ▪; 10. 191 south to 40 east; 11. I-15 south to U.S. 6 south to 191 south to I-70 east; 12. 190

Reading Mileage Charts, page 42
1. 5,938, 2. 5,537, 3. 682, 4. Moscow

Switzerland, Indiana? page 44
1. Posey; 2. Tippecanoe; 3. north;
4. Washington, Lawrence, Monroe, Brown, Bartholomew, Jennings, Scott; 5. Ohio, Orange, Owen; 6. Marion; 7. 10; 8. Michigan, Ohio;
9. southeast

Where Is Switzerland When It's Not in Indiana, page 45

1. Italy, France, Germany, Austria; 2. Adriatic Sea; 3. Warsaw; 4. Finland; 5. west; 6. Copenhagen; 7. Germany; 8. France; 9. Spain

Smalltown, U.S.A., page 50

A. 4, B. 7, C. 12, D. 11, E. 2, F. 9, G. 6, H. 3, I. 13, J. 14, K. 8, L. 1, M. 10, N. 5, O. 15, P. north, Q. west, R. yes, S. no

How High Is Up? page 57

1. 257
2. 1,343
3. 3,427
4. 31
5. 1,050
6. 2,186
7. 1,100
8. 90
9. 1,784
10. 590
11. 185
12. 125
13. 27
14. 200
15. 1,587
16. 25
17. 141
18. 2,050
19. 762
20. 674

A Look at South America, page 63

1. Brazil; 2. Pacific Ocean; 3. Uruguay; 4. south; 5. north; 6. north; 7. Atlantic Ocean; 8. French Guiana; 9. Lima; 10. Ecuador, Colombia, Brazil

Product Maps, page 69

1. WV, 2. L, 3. WV, 4. WV, 5. L, 6. WV, 7. L, 8. L, 9. WV, 10. L, 11. L, 12. L

How Hot Does It Get? page 74

1. 50° to 68°; 2. California, Nevada, Arizona, Texas; 3. Montana, Wyoming, Colorado, South Dakota, Alaska; 4. 68° to 86°; 5. Oklahoma; 6. New Mexico

Would You Like to Buy the Brooklyn Bridge? page 78

Memphis, Camden, Savannah, Clarksville, Nashville, Lebanon, Byrdstown, Kingsport, Morristown, Knoxville, Harriman, Winchester

Know These Terms, page 81

1. Q., 2. T., 3. N., 4. J., 5. G., 6. F., 7. C., 8. K., 9. E., 10. D., 11. H., 12. P., 13. O., 14. S., 15. I., 16. L., 17. A., 18. M., 19. R., 20. B.